# THE EASTER JESUS

# THE EASTER JESUS

GERALD O'COLLINS, S.J.

New Edition

DARTON, LONGMAN & TODD
London

**British Library Cataloguing in Publication Data**

O'Collins, Gerald
The Easter Jesus. – 2nd ed.
1. Jesus Christ – Resurrection
I. Title
232'.5 BT481

ISBN 0–232–51500–X

First published 1973
Second Edition 1980

Darton, Longman & Todd Ltd
89 Lillie Road
London SW6 1UD



ISBN 0 232 51500 X

Printed in Great Britain by The Anchor Press Ltd
and bound by Wm Brendon & Son Ltd
both of Tiptree, Essex

To the faculty and students of Weston College
In gratitude for their creative support and friendship.

We may be Protestants or Catholics, Lutherans or Reformed, to the right or to the left, but in some way we must have seen and heard the angels at the open and empty tomb if we are to be sure of our ground.

Karl Barth, *Church Dogmatics*

# *Contents*

# *Preface*

The discussion of our theme is sometimes initiated by the loud assertion that Christianity stands or falls with the reality of Jesus's resurrection from the dead. That kind of assertion resembles the assurance that at Easter he was 'victorious over death' and 'lives now'. Such statements mask realities so complex that —at least as starting-points—they may prove to be practically worthless. To insist that Christ's resurrection is 'real' does not say very much. What kind of reality are we dealing with? Does the resurrection fall into the class of (past) reality which historians investigate? Is it a (present) reality which affects our personal existence? Does this reality belong rather to the history of ideas?

Likewise, the assertion of Jesus's victory over death leaves much unsaid. The vital question remains unanswered: In what sense did Jesus prove victorious? Did his victory consist in the fact that he kept his principles intact without being deterred even by the fear of execution? Or should we locate his triumph in the rise and spectacular success of the Christian movement? Or was he victorious in being 'raised from the dead' and made 'alive to God' (Romans 6:9f.)? How should we interpret these words of Paul? What kind of life does Jesus now enjoy? May a belief in his resurrection co-exist with the admission that his bones lie somewhere in Palestine? Or is he alive only in the sense in which Beethoven lives for delighted hearers of the Seventh Symphony? It would be folly to pretend that any of these momentous questions can be decided quickly, but decided they must be if our statements about the resurrection are not to remain patently inadequate.

But all questions cannot be raised, let alone answered, together. Which particular question(s) can most usefully initiate our discussion of Christ's resurrection? This raises a further, and to my thinking, quite fundamental point about method. Once we have settled our starting-point, what order shall we choose to follow in our questions? On the one hand, if we undertake to unfold the Church's Easter-faith by setting out its content and motivation, we will begin from a supposedly fixed understanding of the resurrection and an unquestioned affirmation of its (historical?) reality. Such an approach, by presuming answers to the most important questions, inspires little confidence in a post-Enlightenment world. On the other hand, do we gain anything by adopting some neutral standpoint from which we propose to examine the nature of Christ's resurrection and the evidence for it? That would mean starting outside the circle of Easter-faith and scrutinising the (historical?) evidence with the intention—presumably—of justifying faith successfully. In that case the process expressed by the axiom *credo ut intelligam* ('I believe in order that I may understand') would be reversed: *intelligo ut credam* ('I examine the historical evidence from the New Testament in order that I may believe in Christ's resurrection'). Yet we may not side-step the objection that such an allegedly neutral starting-point tries to hide the fact that we actually begin our enquiry as believers (or non-believers) in Jesus's resurrection. Such a pretence of methodological neutrality could serve to make theologians mistrusted.

I cannot, however, rid myself of the suspicion that our choice does not simply lie between beginning *either* within the circle of Easter-faith *or* outside of it. We can accept the option of taking up first the biblical witness to the resurrection and investigating this testimony, while setting to one side for the moment our belief (or unbelief). Our initial aim would be to establish as precisely as possible what Paul and the evangelists affirm and what historical origins lie behind their affirmations. Certainly we would run a considerable risk of allowing present belief or unbelief to affect our reading of the Easter texts. Prior convictions could direct our interpretation. But at least we could attempt to keep such convictions under control and expound the sense of New Testament texts with some objective fidelity.

In these terms our order of questions can be settled. Once the original sense and historical origins of the Easter texts have been clarified, let us put the fundamental question : Can we now accept the apostolic testimony to the resurrection? If that question is answered affirmatively, we will try to offer some theological elucidation of the resurrection. Thus the content of this book can run as follows : Part One will deal with the New Testament testimony, Part Two with the personal acceptance (or rejection) of this testimony, and Part Three with further reflections on the nature of the resurrection.

Recent years have seen a flood of books and articles on Christ's resurrection. This is a welcome swing away from Western Christianity's long-standing preoccupation with Good Friday at the expense of Easter Sunday. Not since the second (and early part of the third) century has the resurrection won such attention from Christian writers. The last half of the twentieth century promises to atone for nearly two thousand years of neglect. At the same time, however, much of the literature on the resurrection offers minute examination of specific passages such as I Corinthians 15 :3–8 and Mark 16 :1–8, or else is engrossed with the elaborate details of debates between scholars, frequently German scholars. This book is offered as a straightforward account of Christ's resurrection from the aspect of history, belief and theology. In many ways its scope resembles that of Willi Marxsen's *The Resurrection of Jesus of Nazareth*,[1] albeit that I strongly disagree both with his overall conclusions and with various subordinate assertions he defends.[2]

There should be no need to dwell on the momentous importance of our theme. The author of First Peter exclaims : 'Blessed be the God and Father of our Lord Jesus Christ! By his great mercy we have been born anew to a living hope through the resurrection of Jesus Christ from the dead' (1 :3). This hope must be dismissed as deluded, if this resurrection of Jesus Christ proves to be no more than wishful thinking on the part of a group of first-century Galileans.

Unless otherwise indicated, the scriptural texts in this book are taken from the Revised Standard Version of the bible, copyrighted 1946 and 1952 by the Division of Christian Education of the National Council of Churches and used by permission.

Finally, I would like to express my sincere thanks to Mrs.

Leonie Hudson and Mrs. Marie Cutler for their care and skill in typing the manuscript.

Weston College School of Theology,
Cambridge, Massachusetts.

[1] Tr. by M. Kohl (London, 1970).
[2] See my review in *Heythrop Journal* 12 (1971), pp. 207–11.

# *Preface to the New Edition*

WHEN PUBLISHERS OFFER the chance of a new edition, authors almost inevitably feel tempted to tinker massively with their original work. In this case, however, economic and other considerations have curbed that temptation and I have contented myself with three things: some necessary corrections to the text, a revised bibliography and this additional preface. Here I want to voice a few comments and misgivings before reacting to some reviews of *The Easter Jesus* (hereafter *EJ*).

In the original preface (p. xii) I expressed my intention to begin by 'taking up first the biblical witness to the resurrection and investigating this testimony, while setting to one side for the moment our belief (or unbelief)'. Since writing that, I have been convinced by H. G. Gadamer and others that the pretence of such a neutral starting-point, even when we are 'merely' studying the historical data available from New Testament texts, is neither possible nor necessary. What we need rather is an awareness of our presuppositions and settled convictions, as well as a readiness to let them be called into question at the appropriate points. See my 'Hans Georg Gadamer and Hans Küng: a Reflection', *Gregorianum* 58 (1977), pp. 564–5, and Chapters 1 and 5 of my forthcoming *Fundamental Theology* (Paulist Press).

On the question of the words attributed to the risen Christ (*EJ*, pp. 26–7), Raymond Brown's views have pushed me into trying to state my position more accurately and, I hope, more convincingly. See *What are they saying about the Resurrection?* (New York, 1978), pp. 51–5.

Then in dealing with Mark 16: 1–8, I followed L. Schenke and others in suggesting that an empty-tomb liturgy of the Christian community in Jerusalem possibly lay behind Mark's text (*EJ*, pp. 41–2). Since *The Easter Jesus* appeared, Edward Schillebeeckx has also accepted this thesis (*Jesus* (London and New York, 1979), pp. 331f.; 701, fn. 31), even if his particular interpretation of the empty tomb and other matters call for challenge. See my review in the *Gregorianum* 61, no. 2 (June, 1980).

In the context of a discussion of the empty tomb, I wrote of 'Paul's silence about the ministry of Jesus' (*EJ*, p. 44). It would have been more to the point to recall the apostle's remarkable silence about key details of Jesus's passion: the betrayal by Judas, the flight of the disciples, Peter's denial, the legal proceedings before the Jewish authorities and Pilate, the location of the crucifixion, and so forth. Here, if anywhere, we might have expected Paul to introduce some historical details. But for him everything else gets swallowed up by that one appalling circumstance to which he consistently returns: Jesus died by crucifixion.

Chapter 6 ('Accepting the Resurrection') could have benefited by some additions. Personal records of people who have come to believe in Christ's resurrection (or lapsed from such belief) would have thrown further light on the issue. Also the Rahnerian themes of 'transcendental' and 'categorical' experience might have found a useful place in that chapter—at least in the related form of transcendental hope and categorical hopes. Apropos of Chapter 6, I was glad to see James Mackey in *Jesus the Man and the Myth* (London and New York, 1979) developing the theme of 'the existential counterpart' to the resurrection (pp. 114f., 117, 120). Both as a term and in its content 'the existential counterpart' resembles 'the existential correlate' which I elaborated as a key element in Easter faith (*EJ*, pp. 69ff.). However, I feel that Mackey emphasises the faith-experience of the original disciples and later Christians in a way that seriously underplays the resurrection of Jesus himself *and* the apostolic testimony to it. Mackey's book is important, and in a later publication I hope to discuss in detail his treatment of the resurrection.

Chapter 9 of *The Easter Jesus* faced the question: What is transformation through resurrection like? *What are they saying about the Resurrection?* takes that discussion further (pp. 68–86). But even then much more needs to be said.

A final personal comment on my book. Sexist language turns up regularly in its pages. Since it would have taken massive surgery to remedy the problem, however, I left the text as it was and tried to do better in *What are they saying about the Resurrection?* and other subsequent writings. Let me now turn to some comments and criticisms that came from reviewers of *The Easter Jesus.*

When analysing the appearance of the risen Christ to Peter, I remarked that it comes 'chronologically first' *in Luke's account* of the events (*EJ*, p. 82). In his review Edgar Dickie reports me as follows:

> The chapters on the Easter Faith and the Easter Theology are more subjective and unfortunately there are times when the conclusions are less innocent than they seem and less than scholarly. For example, the author is concerned and committed to emphasise the priority of Peter. Peter must be 'chronologically first' to see the risen Lord (*Scottish Journal of Theology* 27 (1974), p. 484).

The same reviewer goes on to speak of 'unconscious prejudice', presumably my Petrine/Papal prejudice as a Roman Catholic. Nevertheless, I remain extremely grateful to Dr Dickie for reacting to the section on Peter as Easter witness—not least because of a long-standing puzzle of mine. For years I have been struck by two phenomena, one biblical and the other theological. First, if they deal with the issue, *exegetes of all denominations* seem to be agreed today that the position of Peter in the emerging Church was heavily (but not totally) determined by his being the first *official* witness to Jesus's resurrection. Secondly, *Roman Catholic theologians* never take up this exegetical consensus either as the starting-point or as the key historical datum for their reflections, but head towards Matthew's 'Thou art Peter', John's 'Feed my lambs, feed my sheep', and the whole debate about the promise, conferral and nature of the primacy. In 'Peter as Easter Witness', an article in the January 1981 number of the *Heythrop Journal* I report the exegetical consensus and illustrate the neglect of this theme in Catholic theology.

Both before and after the publication of *The Easter Jesus* I also pointed to the importance of Peter's role as Easter witness.

See 'The Pope and Easter', *America*, April 1, 1972, pp. 359–62 (reprinted in *Faith under Fire* (Melbourne, 1974), pp. 27–30); 'The Easter Witness', *The Tablet*, March 25, 1978, pp. 297–8; *What are they saying about the Resurrection?*, pp. 87–95. But, to my disappointment, so far this theme has failed to draw comments from any writers, except for Dr Dickie and Eric Doyle ('The Future of the Papacy', *Doctrine and Life* 29 (1978), pp. 612–29, at pp. 617–18).

*The Easter Jesus* criticised G. W. H. Lampe for a certain Platonism in his interpretation of the 'post-mortem' destiny of both Jesus and ourselves (p. 94). In his review Professor Lampe seemingly endorses Platonist dualism, leaves aside the bodily transformation of human beings through future resurrection, and contents himself simply with the hope that our souls will live on with God 'while our bodies lie in the dust' (*Epworth Review*, May 1974, pp. 111–12). This review then confirms the very criticism I had made.

Survey articles by J. P. Galvin, W. P. Loewe and R .C. Ware (all listed in the new bibliography) have things to say about *The Easter Jesus.* I would like to take up some remarks by Loewe in 'The Appearances of the Risen Lord: Faith, Fact and Objectivity', *Horizons* 6 (1979), pp. 177–92. His main criticism seems reasonable. Once I characterised the appearances, *on the part of their recipients*, as 'subjective perceptions with some sort of visual component' (Loewe, p. 182), I should have agreed to use the word 'visions' and allow the natural *questions* to arise about the objective and subjective elements in these visions. Nevertheless, this is not to agree to offer 'a psychological account of the experience involved in the Easter appearances' (Loewe, p. 191). The data provided by Paul and the evangelists about the encounters with the risen Jesus are really so minimal that, while we may bring psychological enquiry to bear on the events which originally produced the Easter faith, we cannot say very much, let alone provide some kind of detailed account. Here we risk trying to force answers from insufficient evidence. Hence I continue to reject attempts 'at a psychological *explanation* of the disciples' experience', not because I believe such attempts to threaten necessarily 'the truth-status of the biblical witness' that 'the disciples really encountered the risen Lord' (Loewe, p. 190; italics mine), but because any 'explanation' (as opposed to noting and describing some psychological elements; see *EJ*, p. 31) goes beyond what the data allow. In fact, when Loewe (partly echoing the reflections of R. C. Ware) suggests that in the appearances 'through the psychically-conditioned operation of the disciples' imagination there occurred a process of transformative symbolisation', and that 'through the images and affect in such an experience of "vision", the redemptive self-communication of God in his risen Christ was effectively mediated' (p. 192), has he truly *explained* very much from a *psychological* point of view?

In short, as is clear in my forthcoming *Fundamental Theology*, I am now more willing to *describe* the human experience involved in the risen Christ's appearances to his disciples, and do so partly from a psychological point of view. But I still oppose efforts to *explain* that experience and, above all, any efforts to explain it in merely psychological terms. Let me hasten to add that Loewe does not advocate such a merely psychological explanation.

Loewe rightly approves of Hans Küng's approach to the Easter appearances as encounters in freedom (p. 191), and accepts Walter Kasper's concern to maintain 'a qualitative difference between the originating faith experience [= the appearances to the disciples] and faith experience subsequently mediated by tradition' (p. 190). For what it is worth, perhaps I should note that both these points were already touched on by *The Easter Jesus* (pp. 15f., 72, 80f) before the original publication in 1974 of Küng's *On Being a Christian* and Kasper's *Jesus the Christ*.

In his review of *The Easter Jesus* Lionel Swain observes that in Chapter VI ('Accepting the Resurrection') I was 'applying to the particular case of the resurrection a more general theory of revelation and faith', and regrets that I did not 'mention, let alone stress, the grace aspect of faith at this point' (*The Month* 235 [1974], pp. 585–86). I hope that this omission is remedied in my *Fundamental Theology*. Further, Swain correctly notes that in Mark 16: 6 the significance of the empty tomb concerns the fact that Jesus is alive and not, precisely as such, what happened to his corpse. However, I would insist on *our* right to recognise a sign value in the empty tomb which goes beyond the evangelist's clear intentions: for instance, the empty tomb as expressing the fact that God has begun the work of the new creation in favour of Jesus's crucified remains. A third point. In general I must agree with Swain that Christ is the image to which all human beings are to be conformed (Romans 8:29). But—in the context of the empty tomb and the question of what happened to Jesus's corpse—how far does that conformity to Christ allow us to conclude (in any way that offers *specific* information) that 'all men will be redeemed from death as Jesus was'? Fourthly, Swain states that my dissociation of Colossians from Paul (*EJ*, p. 123) 'would not be endorsed by NT scholars'. Admittedly the Pauline authorship of Colossians wins support from some scholars like W. G. Kümmel and C. F. D. Moule, but others like G. Bornkamm, H. Conzelmann, E. Käsemann and W. Marxsen doubt or reject it. In any case the high value of Colossians in the New Testament canon does not depend on maintaining that St. Paul was its direct author. Finally, Swain rightly objects to my presentation of the eschatology of Wisdom (*EJ*, p. 105). Studies like G. W. E. Nickelsburg's *Resurrection, Immortality and Eternal Life in Intertestamental Judaism* (Cambridge (Mass.) and London, 1972) show how Greek language of immortality expresses what is basically Jewish theology. Hence it is not clear that the book of Wisdom definitely gives *psyche* a 'Greek meaning' and simply accepts the doctrine of an immortal soul. A certain vagueness remains about the *mode* of that eternal life in which the righteous will be vindicated through a post-mortem judgement. Such a life after death could still in some way involve the whole human person.

One last review. I was surprised to find Geoffrey Turner suspecting that I was 'deeply influenced by Pannenberg' (*New Blackfriars* 55 (1974), p. 432). *The Easter Jesus* approvingly quoted Pannenberg's remarks about the novelty (from the point of view of religious history) of the claim for Jesus's resurrection (p. 31), but later disagreed with the German scholar's one-sided stress on the role of historical reason (pp. 63, 68f.). That was all. I would hardly recognise here a deep influence. Another small point. I certainly did not wish to give the impression that I maintain either the status of the ascension as 'an event which was observed and reported' or that there was literally a 'young man in white in the empty tomb' who spoke to the women. In both cases I was trying to elucidate the essential points which Luke and Mark, respectively, intended to communicate to their readers, and was not at those points judging what I took to be the historical facts behind their texts.

Finally, it may be useful to list some other reviews of *The*

*Easter Jesus*: R. E. Brown, *America*, June 15, 1974, pp. 480–1; J. K. Elliott, *Theology* 77 (1974), pp. 612–13; R. H. Fuller, *Interpretation* 29 (1975), pp. 325–6; P. Gaffney, *Review for Religious* 33 (1974), pp. 711–12; S. Laws, *Religious Studies* 10 (1974), pp. 510–11; X. Léon-Dufour, *Recherches de Science Religieuse* 62 (1974), pp. 278–9; R. C. Morgan, *Heythrop Journal* 15 (1974), pp. 338–9; M. Perry, *Journal of Theological Studies* 25 (1974), pp. 495–6; M. Walsh, *The Tablet*, January 19, 1974, p. 57.

To conclude. I would like to express my sincere thanks to those readers who have encouraged me to think that this book will continue to enjoy a viable life into the 1980s.

*The Gregorian University, Rome* GERALD O'COLLINS, S. J.
*Easter Sunday, 1980*

# PART ONE

## *History*

*I*

# *First Corinthians*

THOSE SEEKING TO investigate what the early Christians claim about Jesus's resurrection can reasonably begin with the first witness, St. Paul. I Corinthians 15 :3–8 forms the most valuable single statement about the resurrection provided by the New Testament. Let us take up this passage in detail. Our preliminary aim is to assess historically the apostle's testimony about what happened in the days following Jesus's crucifixion. The passage raises some obvious questions. Where did Paul's testimony originate? What does he mean by the 'appearing' of the risen Christ? How does he interpret 'resurrection'? Where did the time reference ('on the third day in accordance with the scriptures') come from? Does he understand the witnesses to have played some unique and unrepeatable role? In answering such questions our concern at this point remains confined—as far as possible—to the historical investigation of the apostle's evidence. Only after examining his text and further New Testament data may we proceed to face fully the issues involved in the personal appropriation of the Easter proclamation and in its theological elucidation.

## SOURCES FOR PAUL'S TESTIMONY

It may be helpful to set out schematically Paul's passage listing the witnesses to whom the risen Christ appeared. This section from I Corinthians 15 runs as follows:

3 For I delivered to you as of first importance what I also received, *that* Christ DIED for our sins in accordance with the scriptures,

4 *that* he was buried,
*that* he was RAISED on the third day in accordance with the scriptures,
5 and *that* he appeared to Cephas (= Peter),
THEN to the twelve.
6 THEN he appeared to more than five hundred brethren at one time, most of whom are still alive, though some have fallen asleep.
7 THEN he appeared to James,
THEN to all the apostles.
8 LAST OF ALL, as to one untimely born, he appeared also to me.

I Corinthians was apparently written in A.D. 54 or 55—about ten years before the writing of Mark's gospel and less than thirty years after the events reported in chapter fifteen. Jesus was probably crucified in A.D. 30; Paul's conversion to Christianity can be dated in 33. Three years later he visited Jerusalem (Galatians 1 : 18), that is to say, about six years after the events in question.

Paul introduces his testimony to the resurrection with the technical language of early Christian tradition ('I delivered to you what I also received'). The first section (verses 3b–5) looks very much like a pre-Pauline formulation. Various terms are foreign to Paul's normal usage : 'sins', 'was raised' (*egēgertai*), 'in accordance with the scriptures' and 'the twelve'. (For example, the apostle speaks of 'sins' only where he adopts traditional phraseology. In his own usage 'sin' appears in the singular, as a personified force which invades and enslaves man.[1] Paul nowhere else refers to 'the twelve'.) The basic structure for this credal formulation is formed by the verbs 'died' and 'was raised', two key words (both in early tradition and in Paul's letters) to describe Christ's work. This death and resurrection are represented as enjoying both historical and scriptural proof. Historically, the burial (verse 4) establishes the truth of Christ's death, the appearances (verse 5) that of his resurrection. Further, both death and resurrection took place 'in accordance with the scriptures'.

After citing the traditional formula, Paul begins a new construction and from his own information elaborates further appearances of the risen Christ (verses 6–8). He proceeds to comment both on his past persecution of the Church and his subsequent apostolic labours (verses 9–10). He concludes the whole section by indicating that the Corinthians would unquestionably accept the authoritative nature of this common testimony to the resurrection: 'So we preach and so you believed' (verse 11). Paul can take for granted his readers' agreement with the testimony to the resurrection which leading figures in the early Christian community offer. It seems likely that he has listed all the appearances known to him, as he wishes to offer the widest possible basis for witness to the resurrection.

When and where did this tradition about resurrection appearances reach Paul himself? It may have been transmitted to him during his first visit to Jerusalem where he met Peter and James (Galatians 1:18f.). Or perhaps he learned it from the Christians at Antioch or even from the community which he met in Damascus immediately after his conversion. Whatever the circumstances, Paul received this tradition in the thirties or early forties. Verses 3b–5 may be derived from an Aramaic original composed in Palestine. An alternative view holds that Jewish Christians (perhaps in Antioch) created this formula in Greek which betrays Semitic influences. The arguments for a Jerusalem origin have a certain plausibility: the reference to 'Cephas' and 'the twelve' tie the formulation to that city. It is only here that Paul mentions 'the twelve', who enjoyed great significance for the Jerusalem community but beyond that circle seem to have been relatively insignificant (verses 3b–5). A Jerusalem origin would not necessarily rule out composition in Greek. In any case the whole passage (verses 3–7) reflects its primitive origins in that the individual witnesses themselves—and not the Church as such—guarantee the truth of the Easter message. To the traditional material Paul appends a reference to the event which carried the deepest personal importance (verse 8). The experience of 'seeing' the Lord formed the basis both of his conversion to Christianity and of his call to apostleship.

At the outset it is well to note some limitations and peculiarities in Paul's austere formulation. On the one hand, he does not mention the places where Jesus appeared. He fails to indicate (1) that the appearances came as something astonishing to Peter and the rest, (2) that the disciples experienced the initial doubt which the evangelists record of several Easter encounters, and (3) that these experiences produced the kind of complete reversal in attitude which obtained in his own case. In fact he provides no details about any of the episodes, not even any indications of their relative dates. (Does he suppose a gap of several years between the appearance 'to all the apostles' and the appearance 'last of all' to himself?) Unlike the gospels, he reports no words of the risen Christ. He fails to mention either the empty tomb itself or the women who found the tomb empty. (The words 'he was buried' of verse 4 do not *as such* imply an empty tomb. They are not directly linked to 'he was raised', but merely accentuate the preceding 'Christ died'. They underline the reality and apparent finality of death itself. He was really dead and buried; it was from the grave, the realm of the dead, that he was raised.) On the other hand, Paul records some post-resurrection appearances which other New Testament writers do not mention. The gospel accounts remain silent about the appearance to James and to 'more than five hundred brethren at one time'. For the fact that the risen Christ appeared to Cephas (= Peter) alone, we have explicit corroboration only from an incidental verse in Luke (24:34).

In Paul's account Peter and the rest are not alleged to have witnessed the resurrection itself. Their experience consisted in 'seeing' the risen Jesus; on this basis they proclaimed what Paul received—'that he was raised'. The appearances formed the necessary link between the reality of the Easter event and its proclamation. From Paul's list two distinct groups emerge, each headed by an individual. Peter is associated with 'the twelve' (verse 5), James with 'all the apostles' (verse 7). In each case the verb ('he appeared') is used only once and governs two (indirect) objects. The relationship between various groups remains unclear. Does Paul understand 'all the apostles' to form a wider circle than 'the twelve'? (In their Easter stories some gospels speak more accurately of 'the eleven' [Matthew 28:16; Luke 24:9, 33].) From Galatians 1:18 it is clear that one of 'the twelve', Cephas, was counted among the 'apostles'. Although Paul strongly defends his own status as an apostle, he hardly includes himself here among 'all the apostles'. What he says of the 'more than five hundred brethren' not only fails to fit the whole passage stylistically, but also leaves some obscurity. Did these 'brethren' form a group to which neither Peter nor 'the twelve' nor James nor 'all the apostles' belonged? Or should we understand these groups to overlap? Or, as seems likely, does Paul refer to an appearance of the risen Christ at a large meeting of 'brethren' who had come together for worship, but formed no fixed, official group as did, for example, 'the twelve'? We can at least affirm that Paul reports appearances both to individuals (Peter, James and Paul himself) and to groups (the twelve, more than five hundred brethren and all the apostles). While we may not derive from our passage—nor from the gospels—some uniform (traditional) order of Easter appearances, Paul does indicate: (1) that the appearance to Peter preceded all the other appearances (whether to groups or individuals), and (2) that the appearance to Paul himself, as 'something unexpected, exceptional, and abnormal', formed 'an appendix to a series already closed'.[2]

### HE APPEARED

Next I want to discuss in detail three key expressions in I Corinthians 15—'he appeared', 'he was raised', and 'on the third day in accordance with the scriptures'. In our passage we meet four times the technical term for Easter epiphanies, *ōphthē*, which translators normally render 'he appeared'. Earlier in I Corinthians Paul uses another form of the same verb when he gives a personal version of 15:8: 'Am I not an apostle? Have I not *seen* Jesus our Lord?' (9:1). (Here Paul wishes to assert his status as apostle, whereas in 15:8 he refers to his encounter with the risen Christ as part of a broader argument for the reality of the resurrection.) In Galatians 1:12, 16 he comments on this 'seeing' (involved in his conversion and call to apostleship), and calls it 'revelation' (*apokalypsis*), an event which discloses the divine reality. On the grammatical level *ōphthē* can be taken *either* in a straightforward passive sense *or* as carrying a deponent meaning expressed through the passive form. Hence we would translate: (1) 'Christ was seen', or (2) 'Christ appeared, let himself be seen, showed himself'. In the first case the activity would be that of the witnesses; in the second case the action would be initiated by Christ. From Paul's use of *ōphthē* can we draw any conclusions as to the kind of perception involved? In particular, does he imply that the various witnesses literally *saw* the risen Christ?

First of all, the Septuagint (the Greek translation of the Old Testament made perhaps as early as the second century B.C. and used by the first Christians) provides some help towards the interpretation of *ōphthē*. We can detect three relevant categories for the use of this verb. It applies to *things* which were formerly hidden (or at least temporarily invisible) but now come into view. Thus after the flood the mountain tops are 'seen' (Genesis 8:5). Second, the verb is used of *persons* who *freely* allow themselves to be seen (for example, Exodus 23:15; 34:20). Finally, it denotes divine epiphanies. With sovereign freedom God emerges from his radical invisibility and allows himself, his 'glory' or his 'angel' to be seen. We meet examples of this usage in the theophanies to Abraham (Genesis 12:7) and Moses (Exodus 3:2f.). Such episodes not only constitute revelation, but also send some human being on a mission. Although in these divine epiphanies the 'object' disclosed stands in the foreground of interest (and not the subject to whom the disclosure comes), nevertheless, something is seen. Moses, for example, is portrayed as literally 'seeing' that the bush was on fire.

Secondly, the usage of other New Testament authors (who wrote later than Paul) offers some hints. In Mark 9:4 *ōphthē* occurs to report the sudden, astonishing appearance of Elijah (with Moses) in the company of the transfigured Jesus. In Acts the tongues of fire 'appear' at Pentecost (2:3). Finally, John, even if he avoids *ōphthē*, employed other forms of the verb apropos of those who have 'seen' the Lord (20:18, 25, 29). Here to have 'seen' includes the sense of having perceived with one's eyes.

In view of the usage in the Septuagint and the rest of the New Testament, we can suggest the sense in which Paul uses *ōphthē* as a technical term for the resurrection appearances. (1) The appearances, far from being neutral affairs, demand man's involvement, as did the divine epiphanies to Abraham and Moses. The witnesses receive the mission to proclaim the event of the resurrection. (2) Like God in the Old Testament epiphanies, the risen Christ (who can now no longer be experienced as a worldly reality but belongs fully to the divine realm) initiates the episodes. He freely emerges from his hiddenness to show himself where and to whom he wills. (3) These events constitute revelation. (4) The witnesses enjoy a visual experience. The various ways in which both the Septuagint and the New Testament authors use our word indicate some sense of becoming visible. As a technical term *ōphthē* underlines in the first place the objective action of the risen Christ in disclosing himself, but also secondarily implies a subjective perception which includes some kind of visual component. I would, however, part ways with those who wish to interpret the encounters with the risen Christ as 'visions'. This term, with its heavy connotations of modern psychological explanations, ignores the fact that Paul does not concern himself with psychological aspects of the events he reports, still less with raising questions of 'subjective' or 'objective' visions. The appearances constitute confrontations with the reality of the risen Christ, encounters which drive the witnesses to proclamation (verse 11). God's action produces the encounters, just as he raises Christ in accordance with that divine will mirrored in the scriptures (verse 4).

In our passage Paul juxtaposes the various appearances. His account remains silent about possible differences between the appearance to any individual and the appearance to any of the groups listed. In Paul's austere narration all these events stand on the same level. He takes his own encounter with Christ to be (substantially) the same as the 'appearances' to Peter, James and the others listed. Further, any suggestion that Paul intends visions in ecstasy should be demolished. In fact the New Testament records only one such ecstatic vision of the risen Lord, that of the doomed Stephen (Acts 7:55). This vision attributed to the first martyr of the early community (who apparently played an important role in the Gentile mission and the hellenisation of Christianity), is neither listed in I Corinthians 15 nor mentioned elsewhere. Conversely, where we meet ecstatic phenomena in Paul's letters or elsewhere in the New Testament, such phenomena remain unconnected with Easter 'visions'.[3] In fact the Corinthian Christians who apparently prided themselves on their ecstatic endowments are the very ones who need to be reminded of the tradition about post-resurrection encounters with the risen Christ.

## HE WAS RAISED

Our second question concerns the meaning Paul attaches (1) to the verb *egēgertai* ('he was raised') which he quotes here from the tradition, and (2) to his other verb for the resurrection *anistēmi*. The transitive verb *egeirein* (from which *egēgertai*) denotes waking up and rousing from sleep. Used transitively or intransitively, *anistēmi* denotes being put back on one's feet, standing up and being made to stand up. In a transferred sense these verbs apply to waking the dead. Just as a person can be awakened from sleep and rise, so Jesus has been raised. To clarify the (analogical) sense in which Jesus was 'woken', 'made to stand up' or 'stood up', Paul and the traditional material he quotes sometimes add 'from the dead'.[4] Paul also draws our attention to the analogy by adopting the conventional description of the dead as 'those who are asleep' (I Thessalonians 4:13; I Corinthians 15:6), and calling Christ 'the first fruits of those who have fallen asleep' (I Corinthians 15:20).

Paul's language about 'raising' and 'rising' forms an analogical way of speaking about an event which remains hidden from him in its inner nature. Although we shall return to this theme later, we should note that Paul understands the raising of Jesus, as well as the (coming) general resurrection of the dead, not as a mere resuscitation of a corpse but as involving radical transformation. It means returning to a life free from corruption and definitively removed from death (Romans 6:9f.; Philippians 3:21). Man's bodily existence becomes 'glorious', 'spiritual', and transformed in ways which Paul labours to elucidate through various comparisons and negations (I Corinthians 15:35ff.).

### THE THIRD DAY

In our Easter text from I Corinthians Paul appeals to the tradition he received that Christ 'was raised on the third day in accordance with the scriptures' (15:4). Nowhere else does Paul offer a date for the resurrection. This detail raises two lines of questions. How did this dating arise? Was it based on some historical fact(s) or reached by 'deduction' from scripture? Second, does the phrase 'in accordance with the scriptures' qualify simply the resurrection as such? Or is a third-day resurrection declared to be 'in accordance with the scriptures'?

We might seek to settle the date of the resurrection by appealing to Jesus's own predictions that 'the Son of Man' would be killed and 'after three days' would rise again (Mark 8:31; 9:31; 10:33f.). Were these predictions recalled after Easter by the early Christians, accepted as indicating the chronology of the resurrection and transmitted to Paul through the traditional formulation? Or should we rather understand them as prophecies after the event, words placed on the lips of Jesus to suggest that he knew death awaited him in Jerusalem but freely faced it, confident that a triumphant resurrection would follow? Let me set out the three predictions.

> And he began to teach them that the Son of Man must suffer many things, and be rejected by the elders and the chief priests and the scribes, and be killed, and after three days rise again (8:31).
>
> He was teaching his disciples, saying to them, 'The Son of Man will be delivered into the hands of men, and they will kill him; and when he is killed, after three days he will rise (9:31).
>
> And taking the twelve again, he began to tell them what was to happen to him, saying, 'Behold, we are going up to Jerusalem; and the Son of Man will be delivered to the chief priests and the scribes, and they will condemn him to death, and deliver him to the Gentiles; and they will mock him, and spit upon him, and scourge him, and kill him; and after three days he will rise' (10:32–4).

It looks as if the first and the third prediction were at least to an extent elaborated by the early Church—either by Mark himself or by his sources. The precise details ('they will mock him, and spit upon him' etc.) suggest that the wording of the predictions was coloured by the actual events themselves. With suspicious neatness the three-fold prediction punctuates Mark's narrative and relates it to the coming passion. Three times the disciples misunderstand Jesus and three times he invites them to follow him on the path of suffering (8:32ff.; 9:32ff.; 10:35ff.). Could Jesus have made only one prediction of death and resurrection in terms something like the simplest of Mark's three texts (9:31), in which the sole concrete detail is 'after three days'? The fact that neither this verse nor the other predictions express any theological interpretation but assert the mere *fact* of a coming death and resurrection can encourage us to accept at least a simple prediction as coming from the historical Jesus. Sayings wholly created by the early Church would presumably have interpreted theologically the events of Good Friday and Easter Sunday. Perhaps Jesus did announce his imminent death (a tragedy that in any case the growing conflict with the Jerusalem authorities made quite likely), and predicted that his Father would vindicate him through a resurrection 'after three days', meaning within a short time. After the event this prediction became more specific as a resurrection 'after three days', understood chronologically.

Other passages to which we might look are the temple-sayings. Let me quote them in the probable order of composition:

> Some stood up and bore false witness against him, saying, 'We heard him say, "I will destroy this temple that is made with hands, and in three days I will build another, not made with hands" ' (Mark 14:57f.).
>
> False witnesses . . . said, 'This man (sc. Stephen) never ceases to speak words against this holy place and the law; for we have heard him say that this Jesus of Nazareth will destroy this place (sc. the temple), and will change the customs which Moses delivered to us' (Acts 6:13f.).
>
> Many false witnesses came forward. At last two came forward and said, 'This fellow said, "I am able to destroy the temple of God, and to build it in three days" ' (Matthew 26:60f.).
>
> Jesus answered them, 'Destroy this temple, and in three days I will raise it up.' The Jews then said, 'It has taken forty-six years to build this temple, and will you raise it up in three days?' But he spoke of the temple of his body (John 2:19–21).

As stated in our earliest passage (Mark 14:57f.), the saying (attributed to 'false witnesses') does not necessarily refer to the resurrection. Matthew reduces the prediction to a possibility ('I am able'). In his gospel Luke omits the saying but refers to it in Acts as something *still* to be fulfilled. In John the verb 'raise up' has replaced 'rebuild' and the saying has become a resurrection prediction. But originally it seems that the point of Jesus's words was to criticise the temple and its cult and announce that he would replace them soon with something better. We cannot derive the dating of the resurrection from a supposed prediction in his saying about the temple.

Let us come back to the passion predictions in Mark. Whether or not these derive originally from words of Jesus himself, the disciples who are represented as hearing the predictions do not seem to have anticipated the crucifixion even when imminent nor to have expected the resurrection (Luke 24:19–26). Only Matthew's late and probably legendary story of the guard at the tomb clearly indicates that anybody either expected or feared that Jesus might in fact be raised on the third day.

> Next day, that is, after the day of Preparation, the chief priests and the Pharisees gathered before Pilate and said, 'Sir, we remember how that impostor said, while he was still alive, "After three days I will rise again." Therefore order the sepulchre to be made secure until the third day, lest his disciples go and steal him away, and tell the people, "He has risen from the dead," and the last fraud will be worse than the first.' Pilate said to them, 'You have a guard of soldiers; go, make it as secure as you can.' So they went and made the sepulchre secure by sealing the stone and setting a guard (27:62–6).

It is certainly surprising that the enemies of Jesus remembered so clearly a prediction which the disciples seemed to have completely forgotten. The historical elements behind the story appear to be two: all agreed that the tomb was discovered empty on the third day; the enemies of Jesus accused the disciples of having stolen the body.

On balance it seems unlikely that any prediction provided the time sequence for the traditional text (quoted by Paul) that Jesus 'was raised on the third day'. The fact that the first Easter appearance was supposed to have taken place on that day could have given rise to the time sequence, even though—logically—the fact of encounters on the third day did not as such settle the date of the resurrection itself, which was *ex hypothesi* a hidden act of God. Although Paul does not mention it, the discovery of the empty tomb may be the most likely explanation for the time sequence. (The mere fact that Paul fails to record this discovery does not prove that the story was created *after* he composed I Corinthians around A.D. 54 or 55. Mark, while writing about ten years later, could still incorporate an essentially true report, as we will argue later.) Perhaps the dating was also affected by the current belief that after death the soul lingered near the corpse for three days and departed on the fourth day as decay set in. To affirm that Christ rose on the third day would have been a way of asserting that the resurrection took place before his body began to decay. Even if the powers of this world had crucified him, he remained in the hands of the living God and rose before corruption could finally overpower him.

It is notoriously difficult to decide what Old Testament texts were believed to have been fulfilled in Christ's resurrection on the third day. Three texts have often been mentioned. Matthew 12:40 (which reflects Jonah 2:1) runs as follows: 'As Jonah was three days and three nights in the belly of the whale, so will the Son of man be three days and three nights in the heart of the earth.' But a comparison with the Jonah-logion in Luke 11:30 suggests that it originally referred simply to proclamation. Just as Jonah's preaching induced the Ninevites to do penance, so Jesus's word should all the more bring his hearers to belief. In Matthew's text we see later (post-Pauline) Christian reflection interpreting the whole Jonah story, in the conviction that not only Jesus's word constituted the sign but also Jesus himself in his death and resurrection.[5]

Another passage frequently suggested is Hosea 6:1–2: 'Come, let us return to the Lord; for he has torn, that he may heal us; he has stricken and he will bind us up. After two days he will revive us; on the third day he will raise us up, that we may live before him.' In this expression of Israel's hope for national restoration Christians could have seen a prediction of Christ's fate. A serious difficulty, however, remains. If this were the basic proof text, which supported the reference to the 'three days' in the Easter kerygma, it is surprising that neither Paul nor any later New Testament author cites it.

Psalm 16:10 (cited in Acts 2:27; 13:35) seems the most promising passage—at least in the Septuagint version: 'Moreover also my flesh shall rest in hope, because thou wilt not leave my soul in Hades neither wilt thou give thy Holy One to see corruption.' In the midst of his distress the psalmist acknowledges that Yahweh will prove stronger than the power of death. Luke saw that this prayer had remained unfulfilled for the reputed author of the psalms, King David, who had after all fallen through death and corruption into the power of Hades. Christ himself was the one for whom the prayer had been realised. By his resurrection on the third day he had been saved from that corruption which, according to Jewish belief, began on the fourth day. Yet once again I am discouraged from accepting this solution. If Paul (and his source) recognised Psalm 16:10 as fulfilled through Christ's resurrection, why did he fail to mention explicitly this proof text?

We find the most satisfactory solution by unpacking the traditional formula as follows: 'He was raised in accordance with the scriptures (and this resurrection took place) on the third day', the date being derived from the discovery of the empty tomb. This suggestion takes 'in accordance with the scriptures' closely with the verb, not with the phrase 'on the third day'. We are relieved of the task of speculating about biblical texts which the early Christians might have entertained as indicating a 'third-day' resurrection. For Christ's resurrection (and exaltation) *as such* they found strong scriptural 'proof', pre-eminently Psalm 110:1, Psalm 118:22 and Daniel 7:13. These promises were acknowledged to reach fulfilment in his deliverance from death and exaltation to heaven.

### UNIQUE ROLE OF WITNESSES?

We have examined three key elements in I Corinthians 15:3–8: 'he appeared', 'he was raised' and 'on the third day in accordance with the scriptures'. Only by establishing the original sense of our passage can we face and decide on the claims being made. Another question which needs some attention concerns the role played by the witnesses listed by Paul. Does he imply that their experience should be acknowledged as unique and unrepeatable? Or were these post-Easter encounters in his view no different in principle from experiences of the risen Lord which other Christians might later enjoy? This question admits of profitable treatment, only if we first note the existence of two New Testament models which do not involve the official witnesses in exactly the same way.

According to one supposition (a), which lies behind I Corinthians 15:3–8, Jesus went straight from his tomb to heaven and appeared from time to time on earth. In another supposition (b), which Luke-Acts attests, he first returned from the grave to the earth and ascended into heaven only after he had spent some time with the disciples. For this scheme the Easter experiences during the forty days (in which the risen Lord met, spoke and ate with a privileged group) differed fundamentally from all later encounters with him. As portrayed in Acts, not even Paul's Damascus-road experience was on a par with the Emmaus-road encounter. But what of supposition (a)? Does Paul's account in I Corinthians 15 imply that these post-resurrection appearances do not differ essentially from encounters with the risen Christ which subsequent believers may claim to enjoy? It seems that our text eliminates this position. The risen Lord appeared to Paul 'last of all', in an episode which constituted his special apostolic calling and the basis of his proclamation. Paul will lay claim to later (ecstatic) experiences, 'visions and revelations of the Lord' (II Corinthians 12 : 1ff.), but not on the ground that such experiences validate his official role as apostolic witness. If Paul carefully distinguishes these occurrences from the encounters listed in I Corinthians 15 :5–8, he implies that this distinction should *a fortiori* hold true of any encounters between believers and the risen Christ.

### THE VALUE OF I CORINTHIANS 15

Its early nature, as well as its combination of traditional and autobiographical characteristics, makes Paul's list of witnesses the most valuable single piece of testimony provided by the New Testament for the assessment of the resurrection. In I Corinthians 15 Paul feels no need to name any witnesses for the facts of the crucifixion and burial of Jesus (verse 3f.). But for the resurrection he lists many witnesses, both individuals and groups. The Corinthians have heard of and perhaps personally know Peter (I Corinthians 1 : 12), the 'brothers of the Lord' (including James) and the 'apostles' (I Corinthians 9 : 5). When Paul remarks that most of the five hundred brethren are still living (verse 6), one implication is that the Corinthians in the mid-50s could check Paul's witness by questioning members of that large group. Paul's assertion remains susceptible of control by his readers. Hans von Campenhausen argues that if we decide to call into question the reliability of Paul's list of witnesses, logically we should take all other pieces of New Testament testimony as doubtful.[6] It is instructive that Rudolf Bultmann, although he finds Paul's appeal to evidence for the resurrection distasteful, chooses to level his criticism against the apostle's theology rather than against the reliable nature of his witness. He dismisses his statements in I Corinthians as a blameworthy attempt to compel men to believe in the gospel.

> There is . . . one passage where St. Paul tries to prove the miracle of the resurrection by adducing a list of eye-witnesses

> (I Corinthians 15:3–8). But this is a dangerous procedure . . . The resurrection of Jesus cannot be a miraculous proof by which the sceptic might be compelled to believe in Christ.[7]

But here we touch the grounds for faith in the resurrection, an issue to which we return later.

While rightly emphasising the value and early nature of Paul's testimony, we should not side-step the fact that our verses in I Corinthians 15 express or imply various elements of theological interpretation. The passage is certainly not an historical report in the modern sense. At a later stage we will come back to Paul's theology of the resurrection. Here let me simply note that even the crucifixion—assuredly an 'historical fact'—is not merely stated, but is understood as a saving event: 'Christ died for our sins' (verse 3).

This preliminary expedition into the evidence for the resurrection has concerned Paul's testimony to post-resurrection encounters between Christ and various individuals and groups. Difficult questions emerge, once we move on to further relevant New Testament texts. In the light of the apostle's statements, how should we interpret the various Easter traditions in the Gospel accounts? In particular, how do we relate his testimony with the story of the empty tomb?

[1] See Romans, chapters 5–8, *passim.*

[2] C. H. Dodd, *The Founder of Christianity* (London and New York, 1971), p. 181.

[3] See I Corinthians 14:20ff. and Acts 2:3f.

[4] 'God has raised him from the dead' (Romans 10:9); cf. Galatians 1:1. Luke sometimes enlarges his statements of the resurrection a little further; see Acts 2:24ff., 13:34f., 37.

[5] See R. A. Edwards, *The Sign of Jonah* (London, 1971).

[6] *Tradition and Life in the Church*, tr. by A. V. Littledale (London and Philadelphia, 1968), p. 45.

[7] *Kerygma and Myth*, ed. by H. W. Bartsch (London and New York, 1961), p. 39.

## 2

# *Easter in the Gospels*

Even a rapid comparison of the four gospels shows how widely their resurrection stories differ. This stands in striking contrast to the passion narrative, which is more or less uniformly related by all four evangelists. The appendix to Mark (16:9–20), which was added around the beginning of the second century, represents an early attempt at fashioning a concordance of the diverging resurrection reports. Let me draw attention quickly to some conflicts. The differences are so extensive that we cannot effect a unity by reordering supposedly confused reports.

### DIVERGENCES

To begin with, it is difficult to reconcile the whole set of Galilean appearances with the set of Jerusalem appearances. The Galilean appearances belong to Matthew (except for the appearance to women (28:9), Mark (by implication in 16:7) and John (chapter 21). The Jerusalem appearances belong to Luke (and Acts), Matthew 28:9, John 20, and the appendix to Mark (16:9ff.).

Apart from the differing location of the post-resurrection encounters, we meet frequent conflict over details in the four gospels. In John, the corpse of Jesus is anointed after his death (19:39f.), whereas in Luke (23:56; 24:1) and Mark (16:1) the women plan to perform that service on the third day. In Matthew such delayed embalming of a body already buried is ruled out, as the tomb has been officially sealed and guarded; the women visit the tomb for unspecified reasons (28:1). In Mark three women visit the tomb (16:1), in Matthew only two (28:1). In Mark (16:4) and John (20:1) the tomb is already open when the women come, whereas in Matthew just as they arrive an angel moves away the stone blocking the entrance. Mark's one 'young man in a white robe' (16: 5) becomes in Luke 'two men' in 'dazzling apparel' (24:4) who, nevertheless, speak as one. In John the displacement of the angel(s) by Christ himself (already evident in Matthew 28:9f.) is carried further. The Johannine 'angels in white' function not to announce the resurrection but to guard the tomb. They question Mary Magdalene: 'Woman, why are you weeping?' The risen Christ himself gives her a message of his 'ascension' to carry to his 'brethren' (20:12f., 17). We are a long way from the Marcan 'young man' who directs the women to tell the disciples that Christ will 'go before' them into Galilee (16:7).[1]

Luke expressly contradicts Matthew 28:9 and John 20:14ff. by denying that any women had seen Jesus at the tomb (24:22f.). In the third gospel the risen Christ moves towards his ascension (24:51; Acts 1:9) which will terminate his visible presence among men. In Matthew's account, however, Christ, already ascended and exalted, meets his disciples to announce that he will be 'with' them 'to the close of the age' (28:16–20). In John 20:19–23 the risen Christ confers the Spirit, whereas in Luke 24:49 (cf. Acts 1:5) he promises that the Spirit will be given after his departure.

### PROCEDURE

Many apologists have been content to take these and other discrepancies and contradictions as a sign of the essential reliability of the Easter accounts. Inconsistency has been used as an argument for truth. The witnesses to this unique event agree in substance but differ on unimportant detail. Even Karl Barth, who considered apologetics a threat to healthy theology, came dangerously close to such a procedure, when he explained the disorder of the Easter stories as due to the remarkable nature of the event they report. 'The witness of the apostles and evangelists,' he reflected, falls 'into stammering, into contradictions as if from the effect of an earthquake.'[2] This approach, however, risks ignoring vital historical questions about (1) the transmission and development of traditions, not to mention (2) the role of the evangelists themselves in shaping the texts as we have them. Far from simply leaving 'gaps' which could be filled in by additional facts, the variations in the narratives may arise from theological reflection, apologetical interests and similar causes. We may be dealing with conscious editorial modification, not natural confusion. A 'correct' overall account may be neither possible nor necessary.

Our primary task consists in trying to establish how our texts took their present shape. Are the Easter stories in the four gospels literary developments from unelaborated affirmations of the kind represented by I Corinthians 15 :3–8? This would mean that at the beginning of the tradition there existed only the simple claim to have encountered Jesus who had been crucified. What conclusion do we reach about the discovery of the empty tomb as reported in Mark, the source for the accounts offered later by Matthew and Luke? Should we assess this story as wholly a creation of Mark or his sources? Discussion of these and similar questions will prove precarious, unless we first call attention to certain features which with reasonable assurance we can identify and interpret in the gospel stories. In this chapter I plan also to make some initial observations about the development of these stories both in the pre-gospel tradition and through the work of the evangelists themselves. This should lay the ground for facing our central question: What actually happened in the days following Jesus's crucifixion?

## SOME FEATURES

The Easter stories characteristically form relatively short reports, dotted with inconsistent and implausible details. Why do the women who plan to embalm Jesus's corpse fail to remember earlier the obvious fact that their access to the tomb will be blocked by the stone (Mark 16 :3; see 15 :46f)? (In any case their intention to embalm the body does not harmonise with Mark 15 :46, which lacks any suggestion about the burial being incomplete or provisional.) Why do the two disciples on their walk with Jesus to Emmaus fail to notice the marks of the crucifixion in his hands and feet? Seemingly the stranger presents an ordinary appearance, and yet that same evening he frightens the disciples when he manifests himself to them—risen but still showing the marks of the passion in his body (Luke 24 :36ff.). Furthermore, the resurrection stories hardly enjoy a firm link with the passion tradition. Mark, for example, begins his resurrection narrative by listing the women who go to the tomb (16:1), as though he has not just mentioned the women who witness the crucifixion and the burial (15:40, 47). In fact the one verse which deliberately attempts to link passion and resurrection narratives (16:7) serves to highlight their lack of connection. This editorial addition by Mark, along with his earlier addition to the narrative (14:28), suggests that the original passion and burial story contained no reference to the resurrection, the discovery of the empty tomb and the appearances.

The individual encounters with the risen Christ show little or no inter-connection. Self-contained and detached events, they stand separate from one another in time and place. Jesus meets his disciples on a mountain (Matthew 28:16), behind closed doors in Jerusalem (John 20:19) or on the Emmaus road (Luke 24:13ff.). When he comes to them, it is never explained where he comes from or how he comes. While the evangelists always note the beginning of various encounters with the risen Christ, they normally fail to indicate the end of such encounters except by beginning a new pericope. No longer do we see Jesus living in lasting companionship with his disciples. There are only transitory meetings which he himself both begins and terminates.

Unlike the angelic apparitions to Joseph (Matthew 1:20; 2:13, 19f.), none of the Easter appearances is said to have taken place during sleep in a dream. They do not even occur by night, as do several 'revelations' mentioned in Acts (16:9; 18:9; 23:11; 27:23). Nor may these appearances be likened to Peter's vision which, even though it happens by day and when he is awake, takes place in an ecstasy (Acts 10:9ff.). In fact nowhere in the New Testaments are the Easter encounters described as 'visions'. There are no silent encounters; the risen Christ always speaks to those whom he meets. No special stress is placed on the visual components of these encounters with him. The resurrection stories lack the traits of apocalyptic glory found in the Transfiguration narrative (Mark 9:2–8 and par.). Unlike the Matthean angel of the resurrection (28:2–4), the risen Jesus fails to appear with such glory as would compel immediate recognition from men. According to Luke's account of the walk to Emmaus, for several hours two disciples entertain Jesus unawares. As C. F. Evans comments, 'the story is the furthest possible remove from the category of heavenly vision of the Lord in glory'.[3] Luke does not even introduce any 'glorious' details in his description of the ascension.

Finally, the resurrection narratives show some common characteristics: the disciples are in sorrow, bereft of their Lord; he appears, greets them, identifies himself, utters words of comfort and joy, and entrusts to them a missionary charge; after initial doubt the disciples recognise him and rejoice. The appearances may be divided into brief narratives and longer ones. Another classification separates 'mission' appearances to a group of official witnesses (who are entrusted with an apostolic task) from 'personal' appearances. In the latter case some private person recognises Christ and becomes assured of the resurrection (Matthew 28:9f.; Luke 24:13–35; John 20:11–18).

## GALILEE OR JERUSALEM?

Despite some similarities, it is true to say that the gospels record the post-resurrection events in sporadic traditions which, as we have noted, present numerous divergences and contradictions as regards circumstances and witnesses. Should we attempt to harmonise these accounts and produce one consistent story? Take, for instance, the differing geographical location of the risen Christ's appearances. It is possible to reconcile the stories and have the disciples speeding back and forth between Jerusalem and Galilee. After all Matthew, although he favours Galilee, does not deny all Jerusalem appearances (28:9). Conversely, Luke hints perhaps at Galilee appearances in describing the disciples as 'men of Galilee' (Acts 1:11). Hence one could postulate appearances first in Jerusalem (Luke and John chapter 20), then in Galilee (Mark, Matthew, and John chapter 21), and then once again in Jerusalem (Acts chapter 1). 'The eleven' were Galileans. Shortly after the conclusion of the Passover Festival and their meeting with the risen Christ, they would have returned home with other pilgrims from the north. After once again meeting Christ in Galilee, they went back to Jerusalem. The command not to leave Jerusalem (Luke 24:49; Acts 1:4) would have meant: 'Do not this time return to Galilee, as you did after the Passover.'

Such harmonising efforts, however, achieve little. (After all, if someone accepts the truth of the resurrection, what does it matter *where* the risen Christ met his disciples? In his list of resurrection witnesses Paul feels free to dispense with all geographical details.) Attempts at the reconciliation of divergent texts can miss the causes which operated to give our texts their present form and content. If we respect the implication of Mark 16:7 that Galilee formed the historical place of the post-resurrection encounters, then the Jerusalem setting could have arisen through a tendentious desire on the part of the Jerusalem church to locate Christian origins there. Once we accept the historical priority of Galilee, we can see motives at work (both in the developing tradition prior to the gospels and in the theological interests of the evangelists themselves), which could have produced the geographical disparity.

Luke's gospel moves to its climax by its special emphasis on Jesus's 'going up' from Galilee to Jerusalem. The city which formed the centre for past revelation has become the scene of fulfilment. Divine fidelity secures continuity in salvation history. Jerusalem is the place of the temple, the point at which the third epoch of salvation history, the period of the Church, begins. From here the gospel will move out to the whole world. It would spoil Luke's pattern of theological geography to introduce resurrection appearances in Galilee. Hence he deliberately and skilfully changes Mark's injunction ('Tell his disciples and Peter that he is going before you to Galilee; there you will see him, as he told you' (Mark 16:7)). The reference to Galilee becomes a reminiscence of something said in Galilee: 'Remember how he told you, while he was still in Galilee, that the Son of man must be delivered into the hands of sinful men, and be crucified, and on the third day rise' (Luke 24:6f.). For Luke Galilee belongs to the past as something to be remembered.

On the other hand, in the first gospel (which shows itself manifestly antagonistic to the Jewish authorities in Jerusalem) it is natural to find the risen Jesus separating himself from the unbelieving city and returning to Galilee. As leader of the New Israel (19:28), in a scene which recalls the Sermon on the Mount and Moses on Mount Sinai, he sends out his apostles from a mountain into the whole word (28:16–20). Revelation no longer makes Jerusalem its centre, but has moved from there to Galilee and will move from Galilee out to the rest of mankind.

APOLOGETIC TENDENCIES

For a proper appraisal of the Easter accounts, we must hold before our attention not only the conflict between the various gospels but also the apologetic elements that can be detected. To interpret a text as reflecting such interests is, of course, not to foreclose the issue of its historical factuality or falsity. As such it is a judgment about the motivation for its insertion in the story. An evangelist could have used authentic traditions (which originally lacked apologetic tendencies) for his own apologetic purpose. Let me draw attention to three instances. Pilate is represented by Mark as expressing wonder that Jesus was already dead and seeking confirmation from the officer in charge of the execution (15:44). At this point in the text the fact of Jesus's death is being established and officially confirmed. He was not taken down from the cross when he was only apparently dead. The later disappearance of the corpse may not be explained as the revival of an unconscious man. Second, Matthew's account introduces a Roman guard at the tomb to meet the charge that the disciples removed the corpse. The chief priests and Pharisees are portrayed as requesting a guard from Pilate to prevent precisely such a fraud. They refer to Jesus's prediction that he would rise 'after three days', a prediction that is assumed to be common knowledge. The guard will be necessary only 'until the third day' (27:62ff.). After the resurrection some of the soldiers from the guard make a report—not to their superior, Pilate (who had sent them to watch the tomb), but to the Jewish chief priests. The soldiers receive bribes to spread the lying story that the body had been stolen during the night. At this point Christians are assumed to know exactly what went on behind the scenes in Jerusalem (28:11–15). A third example concerns the removal of the stone. We noted above how in the Marcan account women arrive to find Jesus's tomb already open (16:4). In Matthew's account, however, the tomb was not only sealed and guarded, but also in front of the terrified guards an angel of the Lord rolled back the stone and spoke to the women who had just arrived. Robbers (and others) had no chance to enter and remove the corpse before witnesses came on the scene. Later we will examine some apologetic elements special to Luke and John, who betray a strong desire to prove the indubitable corporeal reality of the risen Christ.

These preliminary observations allow us to raise two major issues about the Easter stories in the gospels. Does the story of the discovery of the empty tomb enjoy a factual basis? Second, how reliable are the appearance stories? Have they become so overgrown by legendary elements in the course of transmission or been so embroidered by the evangelists themselves that these stories add nothing of historical value over and above Paul's bald statements in I Corinthians 15:5–8? Was there originally only one resurrection story—either an alleged appearance to Peter or the kind of group episode represented by Matthew 28:16–20—which has then been multiplied? Let us initiate examination of the second issue, reserving for later discussion the issue of the empty tomb stories.

We can divide the stories of Christ's appearances into two groups, (A) those which correspond to appearances mentioned by Paul and (B) those about which he is silent. Besides briefly confirming Paul's reference to the appearance to Peter (Luke 24:34), the gospels report various encounters with 'the twelve' and/or 'all the apostles' (I Corinthians 15:5, 7). In Matthew 'the eleven disciples' (28:16) meet Jesus on a mountain in Galilee; Mark implies that the 'disciples' see Jesus in Galilee (16:7); in Luke Jesus appears to 'the eleven gathered together and those who were with them' (24:33). Group (B) includes such 'personal' appearances as the Emmaus story (Luke 24:13–35) and the appearance to Mary Magdalene (John 20:11–18). Should we accept these stories as enjoying an historical core, although they lack confirmation by Paul and are related in only one gospel? Without question, it would be unjustified to arrive at our conclusions simply by counting the noses of witnesses. But all the same, a post-resurrection appearance to 'the eleven' finds multiple attestation from Paul and the evangelists in a way that the appearance to Cleopas and his companion does not.

We can usefully tackle our problem by isolating one (most important) item which the gospel stories (in the case of Matthew, Luke-Acts and John) add to Paul's testimony—various words of the risen Lord. Paul preserves only one logion of the risen Christ, some words of personal encouragement given to the apostle himself when harassed by his 'thorn in the flesh' (II Corinthians 12:9). But in the gospels Christ commissions 'the eleven disciples' to proclaim and baptise (Matthew 28:18–20), he empowers them to forgive sins (John 20:22f.) and so forth. The words placed on the lips of the risen Lord in one gospel exhibit few and then only approximate parallels in other gospels. In the Easter narratives we find nothing like the close and extensive parallelisms characteristic of the logia which belong to the ministry of Jesus. Should we interpret *all* the words attributed by the gospels to the risen Christ as non-authentic, that is to say never uttered by Christ himself but created either in the course of oral tradition or directly by the evangelists themselves? These words then would interpret the resurrection and its consequences. They would express the significance which the early Christians came to recognise in the Easter appearances and, in particular, their convictions about the world-mission involved in these encounters. Such convictions, formulated as injunctions, appear in the gospels on the lips of Christ himself.

Whatever the factual nature of the appearances, historical authenticity can hardly be claimed for any words attributed to the risen Christ. Even granted that the gospels—or at least the synoptic gospels—are substantially reliable in reporting Jesus's words and deeds during his ministry, we may not without further ado attribute such reliability to the post-resurrection stories. As we have seen, the Easter pericopes describe brief, isolated events, which abound in unexplained, inconsistent and historically implausible details. Second, their subject matter, the episodes following Christ's resurrection, differs dramatically from most events related in the body of the gospels. Third, there is an obvious historical problem created by the fact that all three evangelists who attribute words to the risen Christ represent the mission to the whole world as the immediate issue of the resurrection. If there had been such an explicit command to evangelise mankind, how can we explain the early years in the history of the Church? So far as the evidence from Acts and Paul goes, it seems that at the outset the Christian leaders were scarcely aware of any such command. Convictions about the Church's mission to the whole world were arrived at gradually and then read back into the resurrection narratives. Fourth, the precise words of the risen Christ in Matthew, Luke and John are heavily stamped with the characteristics of each particular evangelist. Matthew, for example, concludes his gospel with what looks very much like his own construction: 'All authority in heaven and on earth has been given to me. Go therefore and make disciples of all nations, baptising them in the name of the Father and of the Son and of the Holy Spirit, teaching them to observe all that I have commanded you; and lo, I am with you always, to the close of the age.' These words take up language and summarise themes of the first gospel in a way which make the section 'a climax and conclusion of Matthew's particular presentation of the gospel material and of the figure of Christ, and which would make it as out of place at the end of any other gospel as it is completely in place here'.[4] In short, Matthew has here moved from historical narrative to theological conclusions. Reflecting both baptismal practice and faith in the exalted Christ's presence at Christian assemblies, he creatively concludes his gospel with the Great Commission.

If the words of the risen Christ prove non-authentic, what overall relationship do the Easter stories in the gospels have to Paul's bald statements in I Corinthians 15:5–8? Could such stories be later expansions of earlier, simpler affirmations (of the kind represented by the passage from Paul)? Two arguments render an affirmative answer suspect. Any theories about the spontaneous growth of appearance stories deserve repudiation, when they fail to recognise that I Corinthians 15:3–8 *could* represent a kerygmatic summary of more or less developed Easter stories. We have many examples within the New Testament of extended narratives which also appear in abbreviated form (for example, Acts 10:34ff.). Paul's austere list of Easter encounters could summarise stories already current in the thirties. There exists no *a priori* reason to suppose that the development must have gone from the simple and unelaborated to the more detailed account.

Second, the fact that the gospels preserve no elaborated stories of appearances to Peter and James surely tells against the hypothesis that all the Easter stories in the gospels freely developed from the kind of simple affirmation represented by I Corinthians 15:5–8. Why do such stories fail to surface in the case of such influential figures as Peter and James?[5] In fact there exists a massive discrepancy between the list given in I Corinthians 15 and the Easter narratives in the gospels. Paul's list, if put in the form of narratives, simply fails to produce the gospel stories. The appearance to 'more than five hundred brethren at one time' remains unaccounted for. The main point of equivalence lies between (1) the appearances to 'the twelve' and then to 'all the apostles' (which Paul records), and (2) the gospel stories about appearances to 'the disciples' or to 'the eleven gathered together and those who were with them'.

Some words of summary are now in order. This preliminary expedition into the testimony from the gospels leaves us with several tentative findings. (1) The sayings attributed to the risen Christ seem to derive from the evangelists and their sources rather than from Christ himself. (2) It remains unproven that the Easter stories in the gospels constitute later expansions of such simpler affirmations as Paul's testimony in I Corinthians 15:5–8. (3) The gospels record two kinds of resurrection encounters: shorter, 'personal' appearances and longer, 'mission' appearances to a group of official witnesses. We are left with the crucial question: How reliable are both these appearance stories and the testimony of Paul? Do these stories and that testimony convey to us what truly happened in the days following Jesus's crucifixion?

[1] We can also contrast Mark's description of the angel in human terms with Matthew's account: 'An angel of the Lord descended from heaven and came and rolled back the stone, and sat upon it. His appearance was like lightning, and his raiment white as snow. And for fear of him the guards trembled and became like dead men' (28:2–4).

[2] *Credo*, tr. by J. S. McNab (London, 1964), p. 100.

[3] *Resurrection and the New Testament* (London, 1970), p. 105. Luke, however, does represent the risen and ascended Christ as manifesting himself in glory to Paul (Acts 9: 1ff. and par.). For the third evangelist this encounter with Paul does not count as one of the Easter appearances; which terminate with the ascension.

[4] *Ibid.*, p. 84. The section contains several characteristic Matthean motifs: 'making disciples', the teaching aspect of the Church's mission and Jesus's function of communicating the new law by his instructions.

[5] Evans comments as follows: 'The appearance to Peter . . . stands at the head of the traditional part of Paul's list, and in view of the primacy of Peter in the church, to which more than one strand in the New Testament bears witness, it could have been expected to hold its place there. The one story which *a priori* one would have expected to survive intact would be that of the Lord's appearance to Peter. But it is not so. By the time of the writing of the gospels it had disappeared, leaving behind no more than an echo, and that not in narrative but in credal form ('The Lord is risen indeed, and has appeared to Simon'), which Luke has some difficulty in attaching as an awkward pendant to his Emmaus story' (*ibid.*, p. 53).

# 3
# *The Historical Foundation*

IN THE PRECEDING chapters we examined in a preliminary fashion those texts which must enter into our assessment of the New Testament claims about Christ's resurrection, I Corinthians 15:3–8 and the Easter narratives contained in the four gospels. What actual events lie behind these texts? Where do we find their historical kernel?

## TWO AUTHENTIC TRADITIONS

Behind these texts, I suggest, lie two originally independent and historically reliable traditions, a tradition of Peter and other disciples encountering the risen Christ (represented in its earliest form by I Corinthians 15:5–8), and a tradition of women discovering Christ's tomb empty (represented in its earliest form by Mark 16:1–8). It seems most plausible to hold that the disciples' encounters with Christ took place in Galilee. They learned of the empty tomb only after their return to Jerusalem. They had in any case played no role either in Jesus's death and burial or in the discovery of the empty tomb.

In Mark's gospel we meet an early attempt to connect the two traditions. The women receive the angel's instruction that the disciples are to go to Galilee where they will see the risen Lord (16:7), an instruction prepared for by an earlier Marcan addition (14:28). In both cases Mark's hand seems clear. Remove both 14:28 and 16:7 from his text, and the passages run on smoothly without these verses. Luke's gospel, written some ten or fifteen years after Mark, shows us the traditions drawing a little closer together. Cleopas tells the stranger that the women's discovery of the empty tomb led several disciples to examine the tomb: 'Some of those who were with us went to the tomb, and found it just as the women had said; but him they did not see' (24:24).[1] When John's gospel is written towards the end of the first century, the two traditions have been almost completely united. The disciples are brought into connection with the crucifixion (19:25–27). That distinctively Johannine pair, Peter and the beloved disciple, visit the empty tomb (20:3–10), and the risen Lord appears to Mary Magdalene at the empty tomb (20:11–18).[2] We can set out in the following way the stages through which the two traditions gradually become more closely associated. Mark records the discovery of the empty tomb, but fails to describe any appearances. Luke reports both the discovery and some appearances, but does not locate any appearances at the tomb. Matthew, however, connects the discovery of the empty tomb with one (briefly reported) appearance to the 'two Marys', who take hold of Jesus's feet and are given a message to his brethren (28:9f.). Finally, John allows an appearance (described at length) to Mary Magdalene alone to take place at the grave; she clings to Jesus who sends her with a message to his brethren. Originally, however, the tradition of encounter with the risen Jesus and the tradition of the empty tomb had been independent.

Behind these traditions stood the self-disclosure of the risen Christ to a number of men and women which brought about their Easter faith and caused them to form the first Christian community. This faith did not arise from the discovery of the empty tomb, but it found in this discovery a confirmation and sign of the reality which had already been revealed. Let us look in detail at the position that is being maintained with respect to the appearances of the risen Lord and the discovery of the empty grave.

## PSYCHOLOGICAL EXPLANATIONS

A full-scale argument in support of the claim that a number of his disciples to their astonishment really encountered Jesus alive after his death would involve a thorough examination of different counter-explanations. By various authors the alleged resurrection of Jesus has been explained as the product of fraud, a mistake, an hallucination, a psychological chain-reaction on the part of men vividly expecting Jesus to rise and so forth. Many of these counter-explanations agree in that they interpret the resurrection on the basis of the inner life of the disciples.[3] Whether merely subjective visions, an unbroken conviction that Jesus's cause must triumph, or some other 'immanent' factor is advanced as the explanation, such views run at once into at least three serious difficulties.

Within the context of late Jewish apocalyptic thought, to claim the resurrection of a single individual before the end of the world was to introduce a quite new element. There existed an expectation that the end of the world would bring a resurrection of *all* the dead along with a general judgment. Neither the disciples nor anyone else expected the resurrection of *one* person alone. Without a new, compelling reason they would not have asserted the individual resurrection of Jesus. We can explain away their proclamation 'Jesus is risen' as the projection of an existing belief only by ignoring the expectations of resurrection which actually existed in first-century Jewish religion. What must be accounted for is the shift from the late Jewish confession of 'Yahweh who will make the dead live' to the Christian confession of the God who has raised Jesus from the dead (Romans 8 : 11; Galatians 1 : 1; II Corinthians 4 : 14, etc.). As Wolfhart Pannenberg puts it, 'the primitive Christian news about the eschatological resurrection of Jesus—with a temporal interval separating it from the universal resurrection of the dead—is, considered from the point of view of the history of religions, something new'.[4]

Those who dismiss the appearances as the projection of the disciples' vivid desire to see Jesus again fail to account for the first appearance(s). What the gospels record seems reasonable and obvious: the crisis of Jesus's arrest and death left the disciples crushed. Only by ignoring this evidence can we give plausibility to some picture of men who preserve quite intact their faith in Jesus's cause, wait for him with feverish enthusiasm and out of their excited imagination create the return of their master. The appearances, once they began, would have generated excited enthusiasm. But such enthusiasm did not exist after Jesus's arrest and prior to his post-resurrection appearances. The various hypotheses which argue that the disciples, despite the death of their leader, retained some vivid faith in him rely heavily on psychological explanations, but prove dubious precisely in such terms.

Thirdly, we ought to discard hypotheses that attribute some experience to Peter which then sets off a quick chain-reaction among men supposedly prone to visions. A gap of several years intervened between the first appearance to Peter and the last appearance to Paul. We lack reliable evidence to plot the chronology of the other episodes. But chain-reaction explanations —in addition to their common (gratuitous) assumption that Jesus's Galilean followers were visionaries by disposition—fail to explain how the appearance to Paul near Damascus took place about three years later than the appearance to Peter (probably in Galilee).

### REDUCTIONIST VIEWS

Closely connected with the 'merely subjective' interpretations of the resurrection testimony are various reductionist accounts which raise issues of meaning. The exponents of these views will, for example, argue that the same Jesus who led men to a right relationship with God in his lifetime continues to do so now by the inspiration and originality of his example. This and no more is the point of 'resurrection-talk'. When Paul and the other witnesses claimed to have encountered Jesus alive after his death, they really meant: 'His words came alive for us, God's grace helped us to see the truth of his cause and with the divine help we intend to continue his mission.' In these terms the stories of the resurrection appearances simply form concrete, pictorial descriptions of changed convictions. Before his crucifixion the disciples had heard Jesus's words, on which they reflected in the light of his death. Their outlook changed, so that they decided to accept fully his message. Essentially, their Easter proclamation amounted to (1) the affirmation of some general principle(s) (for instance, 'love conquers'), which they expressed through symbolic narratives ('God raised Jesus from the dead'), and (2) an invitation to lead a life in accordance with these principles.

Paul van Buren's reflections on the resurrection belong here. For him two things happened to the disciples at Easter. They 'received a new perspective upon Jesus and then upon all things. At the same time, they found that something else had happened to them: they became free with a measure of the freedom which had been Jesus's during his life.' Both as regards the new perspective and the new freedom, 'the decisive event was one which they felt had happened to them'. Infected with his 'contagious' freedom, they were led to follow him in his life for others. Their resurrection language expressed a transaction which had taken place between God and themselves in the light of Jesus's life. Hence 'in saying that *God* raised up Jesus, the disciples indicated that what had happened to them was fundamental to their life and thought'.[5]

The value of such reductionist explanations consists in a helpful reminder of the call to commitment and the fundamental change in conduct which resurrection faith demands. The Easter proclamation does not merely aim at transmitting information. Reductionist interpretations play down the so-called *fides quae* (that which is believed about Christ's resurrection), the cognitive content of the Easter message, in favour of the *fides qua*, the faith by which man responds with personal commitment and becomes a generous disciple of Jesus.

If we take this line, it may seem that we are dealing freely and critically with the New Testament texts, but ultimately our treatment will prove neither useful nor trustworthy. It is not useful, because it declines to face the critical questions about the events following the crucifixion, examine the testimony for the resurrection and make serious truth claims. Only some conviction about the way things are will sustain serious commitment. Many, if not most, people refuse to agree that it is better to be committed than to be rational. Questions cannot be readily evaded. For example, to interpret the resurrection as both an affirmation that 'love conquers' and an invitation to undertake a life based on genuine love demands unpacking. If 'love' means here man's love, the assertion remains patently untrue. Experience unfortunately illustrates too often that human love fails, suffers defeat, and shows itself incapable of meeting effectively the malice or sheer indifference of other men. If the principle asserts that God's love conquers, we must ask: In what sense does (or did) God's love conquer in Jesus's resurrection? Finally we will be forced to enquire how God intervened or failed to intervene in Jesus's own destiny.

The reductionist treatment proves untrustworthy, because it fails to do justice to the New Testament evidence. This holds true, whatever form we give our particular interpretation of the resurrection as a transaction between God and the disciples. We may speak of their appropriation of the values for which Jesus stood, the awakening in their minds of the 'New Being' which they had experienced in Jesus during his lifetime, as their 'infection' with the liberty which characterised Jesus's conduct and so forth. But Paul and the other New Testament witnesses did not use the word 'resurrection' to express some such conclusion, consequence or moral of the events which they had witnessed. They pointed to something which had happened to Jesus of Nazareth himself. In the same breath they reported the crucifixion and the resurrection. For them the resurrection affected Jesus just as personally as did his crucifixion. We misrepresent these New Testament witnesses, if we maintain that Jesus simply rose in the sense that men came to believe in him, love him and share his freedom. The primary purpose of the witnesses was to announce what God had done to Jesus, not to relate (fundamental) religious changes in other men.

Likewise, their concern went beyond merely announcing certain saving values attaching to the name of Jesus. Certainly his significance as Second Adam (Romans 5:12–21), the Messiah authorised by God (Acts 2:36) and the Son of God 'in power' (Romans 1:4) was vitally important for them. But this significance did not, so to speak, hang in the air; it was derived from a real event affecting Jesus himself. He could be so described, because God had intervened to raise him to new life.

### THE APPEARANCES

As the New Testament record stands, no one witnessed or claimed to have witnessed the events of the resurrection itself. It was understood to form the necessary presupposition to the fact that after his crucifixion Jesus appeared alive to Peter, Paul and others. If—unexpectedly—he came and met them, he must have risen from the dead. To maintain that these encounters were objective is to affirm that the encounters produced the disciples' faith and not vice versa.

The question has sometimes been raised: What would a chance passer-by have seen or heard on the occasion of one of these encounters? In modern terms, what would a tape recorder or a camera have preserved for us? We may well be convinced that we must leave indeterminate many details of these experiences. In any case the reality of the resurrection encounters does not depend upon the fact that men could have photographed them. It is enough to be persuaded that the disciples met again him whom they knew to have died.

To some extent our readiness to elaborate on the nature of the encounters with the risen Christ will be governed by the degree of historical reliability which we assign to the triple account given in Acts (9 : 1ff.; 22 : 4ff.; 26 : 9ff.). Here Paul's Damascus-road experience is represented as his meeting a bright light 'from heaven' and hearing a voice. Strictly speaking, Luke does not portray the event as a *vision* of the risen Lord, but as an auditory experience accompanied by light phenomena. Even if we accept the account given in Acts as reliable, there seems to be no effective reason why we should suppose that the other appearances were of precisely the same kind. It is true that in his appeal to the evidence for the resurrection (I Corinthians 15 : 3–8) Paul lists those who encountered the risen Christ, without indicating any differences between their experiences. But it would be a dubious procedure to allege on the basis of this summary formulation that Paul implies that the episodes matched each other in their concrete details. It would prove even more dubious to use I Corinthians 15 : 3–8 to mount an argument that the account in Acts of Paul's conversion typifies the experience of the other resurrection witnesses.

For the purpose of his appeal to the Corinthian Christians Paul takes the various encounters with the risen Christ as enjoying similar status and importance. He does not offer any description of these events, either individually or in general. Even in the report provided by Acts the stress lies on Paul's conversion. There is no attempt to satisfy the curious questioner who would wish to know details of the risen Lord's appearance. In both Acts and I Corinthians (as well as in Galatians chapter 1) the encounters with the risen Christ operate to establish the reality of the resurrection and to communicate Paul's missionary vocation. I suspect that in Acts, Luke could not afford to introduce an Emmaus-style meeting on the Damascus road. He has already described how the risen Christ is withdrawn from such contact through the Ascension. Hence the meeting with Paul occurs without any sense perception of the physical form of a man. Nor does Paul enjoy a heavenly vision in the style of the doomed Stephen, who —in a unique episode—proclaims that he sees the heavens opened and 'the Son of Man' (not explicitly identified with the risen Christ) 'standing at the right hand of God' (Acts 7:56).

## GALILEE OR JERUSALEM?

A minor point in the position being maintained vis-à-vis the Easter appearances is that they took place in Galilee and not in Jerusalem (as represented by Luke-Acts and John 20). After Jesus's arrest (and death), when the disciples abandoned his cause, did they hide themselves in Jerusalem or leave at once for Galilee, the home of many, if not all, of them? Obviously Mark's account of the arrest in Gethsemane ('they all forsook him, and fled'—14:50) does not necessarily indicate a flight back to Galilee. In fact, both the Galilee (Mark and Matthew) and Jerusalem (Luke and John 20) traditions agree in supposing that at least up to the Easter day itself Jesus's disciples were still in Jerusalem and that a flight from the city had not taken place immediately after the crucifixion.

If it is agreed that the disciples returned to Galilee where the appearances occurred, we can suppose either (1) that they fled there in fear after Jesus's arrest and crucifixion,[6] or (2) that along with other Galilean pilgrims to the Passover festival they had to go home after some time,[7] or (3) that they were given cause to return home by the discovery of the empty tomb.[8] Hypotheses (1) and (2) would both make the departure for Galilee independent of the discovery of the empty tomb.

Many scholars have followed Rudolf Bultmann's position. The oral tradition told of a flight to Galilee, but this was deleted in Mark's account. Hence the evangelist inserts into the traditional material 'footnotes' (14:28 and 16:7), which prepare the way for one or more Galilean appearances. The disciples go to Galilee on the basis of a command. The lost ending of Mark's gospel, if there were such, would have recorded the meeting(s) with the risen Christ in Galilee. The Bultmann view offers a neat solution.

However, a serious problem arises from the meaning of 'Galilee' in Mark. Since the 1930s, it has been recognised that the second evangelist does not always use 'Galilee' in a merely geographical sense. Frequently the word seems to function as a theological term denoting 'the place of preaching' or perhaps 'the land of the gentiles' symbolising the Church's world-wide mission. This confuses the issue, as Mark 16:7 constitutes the main argument for locating the appearances in Galilee. (Matthew is dependent upon Mark at this point.) What then if Mark uses 'Galilee' in 16:7 as a theological term and not in a straightforward geographical sense? Our alternative would be to accept the Jerusalem location reported in Luke 24. Yet, as we have seen, 'Jerusalem' has a massive theological significance for Luke. Add too the fact that chronological considerations also require that Luke 24 (as well as John 20) place the appearances in Jerusalem. In his gospel Luke fits both the discovery of the empty tomb and the appearances into a single day; John allows for one week. In both cases demands of narrative unity cannot permit a return to Galilee.

Perhaps we must leave unresolved the question of the original geographical location for the appearances. But on balance it looks more plausible to follow Mark (even if he may give a certain theological value to the place of Galilee), rather than Luke who seems to have altered Mark's text for heavily theological reasons and not the sake of historical accuracy.

One explanation of Mark 16:7 ('he is going before you to Galilee; there you will see him') which can in any case be ruled out is that offered by Willi Marxsen, who takes up some earlier suggestions by Ernst Lohmeyer. In Marxsen's view this verse along with 14:28 refers to the *parousia*, which Mark expects to occur soon in Galilee, the land of eschatological fulfilment. When Mark writes in the 60s, he wishes to direct the Christian community to gather in Galilee for the glorious coming of the Lord. Unlike the *ōphthē* ('he appeared') of I Corinthians 15, which is a technical term for *resurrection* appearances, the *opsesthe* ('you will see') of Mark 16:7 points to the *parousia*.[9]

A number of considerations tell against this view. Marxsen takes 'Galilee' in the rest of Mark's gospel to be a theological term denoting the place of preaching. He must suppose that in 14:28 and 16:7 it reverts to the status of a geographical term. Second, from the rest of his gospel it is not clear that Mark anticipates an imminent *parousia*. Third, other evidence is lacking to establish sufficiently any special connection between Galilee and the *parousia*. Fourth, Mark presents the predictions of the Son of Man's passion and resurrection (8:31; 9:31; 10:32–4) separately from passages which can be interpreted as conveying—among other things—predictions of the *parousia* (chapter 13).

Elsewhere in his gospel Mark keeps the themes of resurrection and *parousia* apart. It is hardly to be expected that he will mix them in chapter 16 by combining an announcement of an imminent *parousia* (to occur in the late 60s) with an account of women on Easter day (more than thirty years before) discovering the tomb of the risen Christ to be empty. Fifth, we can interpret the words 'he is going before you to Galilee' in two ways: either (1) 'he is going *at your head* (like a shepherd leading his sheep) to Galilee', or (2) 'he is going *in advance of you* with a view to a rendezvous in Galilee'. Explanation (1) seems more likely, inasmuch as it picks up the theme of 14:27ff., the apostasy of the twelve and of Peter in particular. The shepherd's flock will be scattered, but this process will be reversed when the flock is re-assembled. In either case the 'going before' as such does not evoke any thoughts of the *parousia*. Finally, Marxsen himself has become considerably more tentative about his view that Mark 16:7 points to an imminent *parousia* rather than an imminent post-resurrection appearance.[10]

## THE EMPTY TOMB

Much more important than any conclusion about the geographical setting of the Easter appearances is the issue of the empty tomb. At the beginning of this chapter the claim was made that Mark's account of women discovering Jesus's tomb to be empty derives from a true historical episode. This story has, of course, often been interpreted as a non-historical legend, a pictorial form in which some early Christians preached the resurrection without intending the story to be taken as an historical account.[11] Many would strike out the empty-tomb tradition as part of a total rejection of the claim that God raised Jesus from the dead. Others again dispense with this tradition as a secondary historicisation of the original Easter message, while accepting as objectively genuine the tradition of the Easter appearances. In this view Jesus truly lives with God, even though his crucified body decayed in the grave and his bones lie somewhere in Palestine.[12] On whatever grounds, may we then repudiate the authentic historicity of the empty-tomb tradition? In my opinion, this would amount to tampering seriously and unnecessarily with the early Christian witness to the resurrection. On the available evidence the substantial factuality of the empty-tomb tradition has much to be said for it and no convincing argument against it. What part this tradition should play in an adequate Easter faith and theology remains another question. In this chapter we examine simply the issue of historical truth.

As Matthew and Luke draw on Mark up to 16:8, any discussion of the empty tomb must centre on the second evangelist's account of both the burial of Jesus and the discovery of his empty grave. Some scholars have rejected the empty-tomb tradition by repudiating the whole burial story as a secondary invention. In their view the body of Jesus was burned or thrown into a common grave. There would have been no private tomb for women to visit on the third day or any other day. Thus Hans Grass takes up a vague suggestion in Acts 13:27–9 that Jesus's *enemies* buried him:

> Those who live in Jerusalem and their rulers, because they did not recognise him nor understand the utterances of the prophets which are read every sabbath, fulfilled these by condemning him. Though they could charge him with nothing deserving death, yet they asked Pilate to have him killed. And when they had fulfilled all that was written of him, they took him down from the tree, and laid him in a tomb.

Grass concludes from this that, 'as happened with those who were executed, Jesus was laid in a common grave'.[13] On these grounds the story of Joseph of Arimathea's intervention becomes a later invention. Jesus's burial by his enemies was changed into burial by a kindly outsider. This argument, however, wrongly takes the section from Acts as a reliable source. The very next verses (13:30f.) represent Paul not as appealing to his own encounter with the risen Christ but as relying exclusively on other witnesses to the resurrection! As Luke fails in this speech to portray accurately the historical Paul, we can hardly insist on the strict reliability of a vague remark about Jesus's burial.[14]

Mark (followed by Matthew and Luke) ties the story of Jesus's burial firmly to the name of Joseph of Arimathea. We have no effective reason for denying this account. Attempts to reduce the man from Arimathea to a legendary or symbolic figure do not appear plausible. He was remembered in the Christian tradition simply for his act in providing burial for the crucified Jesus. Roman law relating to the burial of the dead left room for compassion. Sometimes authorities showed themselves ready to hand over to friends and relatives the body of an executed criminal. Joseph of Arimathea's action in approaching Pilate and boldly asking for the body (Mark 15:43) might not have been quite so courageous as the evangelist suggests. From Roman practice Joseph may have had little doubt that this request would be granted, especially as he was a respected member of the Sanhedrin. A recent discovery in rock-cut family tombs to the north of Jerusalem serves to confirm the possibility of compassionate Roman practice. Ossuary four of Tomb I contained the skeletal remains of a young man who had been crucified in the first century A.D. some time before the outbreak of the first Jewish revolt. Despite his crucifixion by the Romans, his bones could be carefully preserved in an honourable fashion.[15]

Any proper analysis of Mark 16:1–8 requires decisions about the evangelist's own contributions to the passage. To note that some passage does not derive from tradition but has been composed by the evangelist himself does not, of course, automatically mean that he has created the *content* of that passage *de novo*. Let me use italics to set out what appear to be his editorial additions to the tradition:

> And *when the sabbath was past*, Mary Magdalene, and Mary the mother of James, and Salome *bought spices, so that they might go and anoint him. And very early* on the first day of the week *they* went to the tomb when the sun had risen. *And they were saying to one another, 'Who will roll away the stone for us from the door of the tomb?'* And *looking up*, they saw that the stone was rolled back; *for it was very large*. And entering *the tomb*, they saw a young man sitting on the right hand, dressed in a white robe; and they were amazed. And he said to them, 'Do not be amazed; you seek Jesus of Nazareth, who was crucified. He has risen, he is not here; see the place where they laid him. *But go, tell his disciples and Peter that he is going before you to Galilee, there you will see him, as he told you.*' And they went out and fled from the tomb; for trembling and astonishment had come upon them; *and they said nothing to any one, for they were afraid.*

It would take us too far afield to set out all the arguments involved in such a differentiation between the pre-Marcan tradition and the evangelist's own work as editor. But a few points must be made. Mark introduces the women's plan to anoint the body as a means of providing motivation for their visit to the tomb. On the way their concern about the stone (which—logically—they should have remembered earlier, as they had been present at the burial) heightens the dramatic effect and prepares the reader for the astonishing message of the resurrection.

With regard to Mark's intentions, the conflict between the silence (verse 8) and the command to speak (verse 7) constitutes a classic problem. Perhaps, as von Campenhausen has maintained, the women's silence expresses the fact that the disciples had nothing to do with the empty tomb. Or else, despite the injunction of verse 7, the evangelist portrays the women as remaining silent, because he (and/or his source) knows that these women could not pass on the message, since the disciples had already returned to Galilee. A third explanation takes up a theological point. Despite the command to speak, Mark insists on astonished silence as the only appropriate reaction to what has been announced. The message of the resurrection plunges the women into such a fright that they are—rightly—struck dumb. They are stupefied at this unique manifestation of divine power. Finally, the conflict may express that tension between disclosure and concealment which characterises the Marcan view of revelation. Here the tradition reports the silence motif, to which the evangelist prefixes the command to speak.

Once the evangelist's editorial additions have been separated from the pre-Marcan tradition, the question arises: What function did this traditional material serve in the life of the early Church? The best available interpretation connects it with an empty-tomb liturgy of the Christian community in Jerusalem. Either annually or more frequently the mother Church would have celebrated the resurrection with a service at the Lord's empty tomb. First-century Judaism and early Christianity have left considerable evidence to demonstrate popular interest in the graves of holy persons. Veneration for the real or presumed tombs of prophets forms the background to Jesus's words in Luke 11:47: 'You build the tombs of the prophets whom your fathers killed.' There is nothing unlikely about Jesus's empty tomb being venerated by believers who either lived in Jerusalem or came there on pilgrimage. The evidence from Acts and Paul's letters shows how early Christians were strongly interested in and visited the mother Church in Jerusalem. For these first Christians the tomb of Jesus was more than the last resting-place of a mere martyr or prophet. It was the place which had witnessed the mystery of God's final saving act. The tradition behind Mark 16:1–8 can be most plausibly explained as the (annual?) liturgical celebration at Jesus's empty and open tomb. The Jerusalem community (perhaps at dawn) met to worship there in remembrance of the first visit on Easter morning.[16]

What of the *dramatis personae* in our passage from Mark—the angel and the women? Nowhere else in the second gospel does an angel take the independent role here assigned to the 'young man'. (Parallels can be found where angels appear as young men and wear clothing conventional for such heavenly beings (cf. II Maccabees 3:26, 33).) Mark's angel has a message to deliver: 'He has risen, he is not here.' The angel does not supply an answer to the question: Who moved the stone? In adapting Mark's text, Matthew (unlike Luke) supplies the answer: 'An angel of the Lord descended from heaven and came and rolled back the stone, and sat upon it' (28:2). Do we leave Mark's angel to play a role in the original event when one or more women found the tomb empty on the third day? Or does it seem that the messenger angel later entered the story as a means of pointing to the meaning of that discovery? The latter view becomes more likely when we reflect that the extremely simple version given in John 20:1–2 could conceivably represent the earliest form of the story: 'Now on the first day of the week Mary Magdalene came to the tomb early, while it was still dark, and saw that the stone had been taken away from the tomb. So she ran, and went to Simon Peter and the other disciple, the one whom Jesus loved, and said to them, "They have taken the Lord out of the tomb, and *we* (Mary Magdalene and another woman or other women?)[17] do not know where they have laid him".' Only Mary Magdalene's name is common to all four gospels. In the original tradition she may have been the sole visitor to the tomb.

Crucial to any evaluation of the historical reliability of the empty-tomb tradition is the place of a woman or women in the story. Surprisingly, women enjoy a witness function in both the passion and resurrection narratives (Mark 15:40, 47; 16:1). By seeing where Jesus was laid, they could testify both to the fact of his burial and the location of his grave. Subsequently they discover that grave to be empty. If this discovery story were simply a legend created by early Christians, it remains difficult to explain why women find a place in the story. In Jewish society they did not count as valid witnesses. For legend-makers the natural thing would have been to have pictured Peter and other (male) disciples as having found the tomb empty. But in the oldest tradition the disciples have nothing to do with Jesus's crucifixion, burial and the discovery of the empty tomb. The role of women in the story provides a sound argument for its historical reliability.

It can also be argued that at least in Jerusalem itself the preaching of Christ's resurrection would not have lasted five minutes, if friend or foe could have produced his body from the tomb outside the city. This would have effectively silenced the apostolic proclamation that God had raised Jesus from the dead. Finally, Jewish polemic against the resurrection supposed that the tomb was known and was empty. Various counter-explanations were offered: the disciples had stolen the body; a gardener had removed it. But the opponents agreed with the Christians on the basic fact that the body was gone.[18]

The silence of Paul has sometimes been invoked as an argument against the historical truth of the tradition concerning the empty tomb. He refers only to the burial of Jesus (I Corinthians 15:4). Just because Mark writes later than Paul and Paul nowhere shows clearly that he knows the story of the empty tomb, we cannot conclude that the story itself *arose after Paul*. The relative dates for the composition of the two works in question, I Corinthians and Mark's gospel, provide no necessary indication for dating the origins of their contents. But what of Paul's proclamation of Jesus's resurrection? Can this at least be reconciled with a denial of the empty tomb? Should we even use Paul to make our stand against the gospel tradition of women finding Jesus's grave open and empty?

In I Corinthians 15 Paul attests that the appearances (and not the fact of an empty grave) create Easter-faith. This does not differentiate his position from that of Mark. In Mark 16:1–8 the three women who find the grave open and empty must hear the resurrection message ('He has risen, he is not here') before their discovery is clarified. Further, what Paul says about the risen body (I Corinthians 15:35ff.) is far from contradicting the tradition of the empty grave. His account of the risen body would be ruled out, if Jesus's corpse had still been in the grave. He maintains a reversal of death and entombment, a *transformation* of our mortal bodies, not the (creation and) *substitution* of brand-new risen bodies. For Paul to assert that God has raised Jesus from the dead necessarily implies a passage from the tomb—however difficult it may be to imagine such.

Some scholars have explained the silence of Paul as deliberate. Although he knew the Jerusalem tradition of the empty grave, he had good reasons for not mentioning it as part of his argument in I Corinthians 15. The disappearance of the corpse established neither the fact of the resurrection nor the nature of the risen body. As such the discovery of the empty tomb remained an ambiguous episode. Second, if the women involved in this discovery were not ruled out as invalid witnesses for the Corinthians, at least they rated as highly inferior witnesses when compared with Peter and the others whom Paul cited as testifying to encounters with the risen Christ. Third, to mention an empty tomb far away in Jerusalem and one or two women witnesses (still alive and dwelling in Jerusalem?) would have left Paul on shaky grounds. By and large such testimony and evidence remained inaccessible for the Corinthian Christians. Paul preferred to remind his congregation of those many witnesses who had seen the risen Lord. Some of these witnesses were personally known to members of the Church in Corinth. Finally, Paul himself had seen the risen Christ, but had not been involved at his crucifixion or burial. The discovery of the empty tomb and its implications for faith would have enjoyed less importance for Paul than for those who were with Jesus from the start and had experienced the traumatic events of his arrest, condemnation and execution.

We may perhaps conclude that Paul knew the empty-tomb tradition, although this remains a highly tentative conclusion, related to the larger problem of Paul's silence about the ministry of Jesus. What is certain, however, is that we ought not to exaggerate the significance of the empty tomb. The evangelists show themselves quite conscious of the fact that as such an empty tomb remains ambiguous and does not compel faith. In Mark's account the discovery of the empty tomb, so far from inducing faith, leads to terrified and silent flight (16:8). Only the appearances of the risen Christ can give this discovery its clear meaning.

[1] I do not read Luke 24:12 as part of the original text.

[2] We can express this growing unification of the traditions by noting the tendency in Luke and John not only to locate appearances in Jerusalem, but also to have them occur on the same day as the discovery of the empty tomb.

[3] In his classic work Wilhelm Bousset formulated such a 'psychological' explanation as follows: 'The faith in the exaltation of the Son of Man acquired the tangible form that Jesus had awakened (arisen) from the tomb on the third day' (*Kyrios Christos*, tr. J. E. Steely (Nashville, 1970), p. 106).

[4] *Jesus—God and Man*, tr. L. L. Wilkins and D. A. Priebe (London and Philadelphia, 1968), p. 96.

[5] *The Secular Meaning of the Gospel* (London and New York, 1963), pp. 133., 169f.

[6] R. Bultmann, *The History of the Synoptic Tradition*, tr. J. Marsh (Oxford, 1968), p. 285f.

[7] See C. F. D. Moule, 'The Post-Resurrection Appearances in the Light of Festival Pilgrimages', *New Testament Studies* 4 (1957–8), pp. 58–61.

[8] Von Campenhausen, *Tradition and Life in the Church*, p. 83f.

[9] *Mark the Evangelist* (London and Nashville, 1969), pp. 75ff.

[10] *The Resurrection of Jesus of Nazareth*, p. 163f.; *Introduction to the New Testament*, tr. G. Buswell (London and Philadelphia, 1968), p. 141f. R. H. Fuller adds an important consideration: 'The decisive argument which proves it to be, in Mark 16:7, a resurrection rather than a parousia reference is the naming of Peter as well as the disciples, a circumstance which indicates clearly that the Evangelist is alluding to the two appearances listed in I Corinthians 15:5. If Mark 16:7 were pointing forward to the parousia it is hard to see why Peter should be singled out for special mention. But if it points to resurrection appearances, the reason for the mention of Peter is obvious' (*The Formation of the Resurrection Narratives* (London and New York, 1971), p. 63f.).

[11] W. Marxsen, *The Resurrection of Jesus of Nazareth*, p. 161; L. Evely, *The Gospels Without Myth* (New York, 1971), p. 84.

[12] So G. W. H. Lampe, in *The Resurrection*, a dialogue with D. M. MacKinnon (London and Philadelphia, 1967).

[13] *Ostergeschehen und Osterberichte* (2nd ed., 1962), p. 180.

[14] J. Blank, *Jesus und Paulus* (Munich, 1968), pp. 34ff.

[15] See V. Tzaferis and N. Haas, *Israel Exploration Journal* 20 (1970), pp. 18–32, 38–59.

[16] L. Schenke, *Auferstehungsverkündigung und leeres Grab* (Stuttgart, 1968).

[17] The 'we' may betray the influence of Galilean Aramaic, in which 'we' could be substituted for 'I'.

[18] See von Campenhausen, *Tradition and Life in the Church*, pp. 66ff.

# 4

# *Resurrection and Exaltation*

THE FIRST THREE chapters of this book examined the nature and genesis of the New Testament evidence for Christ's resurrection. The overall aim was to clarify the astounding claim which the first Christians made about Christ's destiny beyond death. Before investigating what is involved in accepting or rejecting this claim, its content and character must be settled—at least in a provisional fashion. It would not be feasible to discuss here all the problems which could be raised in clarifying the New Testament claim about Christ's resurrection. But two points must be briefly considered, if this treatment is not to remain patently inadequate—(1) the apparent unimportance of the resurrection at certain levels in the New Testament, and (2) the problematic relationship between Christ's resurrection and exaltation. Does a certain neglect of the resurrection in the New Testament throw doubt on the extent and value of early Christian testimony? Should we even *derive* the resurrection proclamation from prior assertions about Christ being 'exalted' and 'ascending into heaven'? Such a derivation would rule out our reconstruction of the origin of the testimony offered by Paul and the evangelists.

## NEGLECT OF THE RESURRECTION

It has been regularly argued that Christ's resurrection constitutes the central affirmation of the New Testament. Whether we accept this affirmation or not, it purports to be the heart of the early Christian message. Yet we may not ignore some contrary data. It seems surprising that—given the importance of the resurrection—the Easter narratives should form relatively brief sections in the gospels. If resurrection faith enjoys a centrality in the New Testament, this centrality stands in marked contrast with the almost fortuitous character of the traditions which support it. Matthew devotes only one brief chapter (twenty verses long) out of twenty-eight to the Easter story. Luke's gospel proves only a little more generous. Further, some New Testament writings (II Thessalonians, Titus, Philemon, III John, II Peter, Jude and James) fail to refer to Christ's resurrection at all.

If the evangelists and some other New Testament authors leave us with a problem, the ministry of Jesus himself sharpens this problem. The theme of resurrection hardly surfaces in his preaching. We see him bent on proclaiming the nearness of God's rule which calls for man's sincere and total obedience. The resurrection appears largely absent from Jesus's concerns, but in this regard he differs little from his Old Testament background. Belief in resurrection emerged late in the history of Israel, perhaps as late as Daniel and Second Maccabees. During the Maccabean revolt against Syria (166 B.C. and later) the doctrine of the resurrection developed with the doctrine of martyrdom. Throughout most of the Old Testament the Israelites seemingly remained content with the traditional idea of Sheol as the place where the 'shades' of the departed dwelt and where life was hardly worth living. There is little explicit teaching on the resurrection in the Old Testament.

Some recent studies have attempted to push back to the pre-exilic period the origins of Israelite belief in life for the whole man beyond death. Perhaps such studies will change the established consensus and bring agreement that a doctrine of resurrection—or at least some unspecified assertion of personal afterlife for the whole man—goes back much further in the Old Testament than has been commonly supposed. Nevertheless, no one can claim that Old Testament authors devote much attention to the topic of resurrection. Nor should we forget that by the time of Jesus the Sadducees, unlike the Pharisees, still refused to accept belief in resurrection, on the grounds that such belief was something new and alien to traditional Judaism. In short, a theme which hardly concerns Jesus and was not firmly fixed in Judaism seems to have moved from the circumference to the centre of Christian faith.

Various solutions can be offered to this problem. One line of approach stresses the self-restraint of the New Testament authors. Despite the overwhelming importance of the resurrection, little data was available about the encounters between the risen Christ and his disciples. Yet the evangelists (and their sources) largely declined to expand or invent narratives dealing with the post-crucifixion days. Thus the problem created by the relatively small amount of resurrection material becomes the occasion of praising the evangelists (and their sources) for sobriety and trustworthiness. Secondly, we need to remind ourselves that the early Christians showed themselves much more interested in who Jesus *is* than in who he was. They acknowledged and valued the presence of the risen Lord rather than detailed information about the first Easter-days. Without feeling that this was odd, they held unswervingly to the centrality of the resurrection and remained undismayed at brief Easter narratives in the gospels. In any case, these brief stories threw a new light onto all that was to be said about the earthly Jesus.

However useful we judge these two approaches, further elucidation is necessary. At many levels we find the New Testament 'ragged'. It lacks finish and often offers little information in the face of urgent questions. How widely was Paul's theology known and appreciated? Do the so-called Catholic epistles mirror more accurately the attitudes of most early Christians? What kind of relationship(s) did the early communities have with Jewish synagogues around the Mediterranean world? What did the early Christian missionaries—apart from Paul—achieve? From our standpoint the New Testament frequently fails to answer important questions and get its emphases and proportions right. Christ's resurrection constitutes another case in point. The proclamation of his resurrection enjoys a pre-eminence, without the New Testament authors feeling themselves obliged to allot it quantitatively more verses than other themes.

By any reckoning we should also attend to the shift between the situation of the historical Jesus himself and that of the apostle Paul. There exists a fundamental difference between (1) the period of Jesus's life and preaching and (2) the period of Paul's mission. This difference determines how explicit and prominent the affirmation of the resurrection will be at various points in the New Testament—above all in the Synoptic gospels (our main source of information about the historical Jesus) and in the letters of Paul.

First things first. Paul does not repeat Jesus's preaching. He believes and announces that at Calvary the last age of world history has already begun. For 'Jesus our Lord . . . was put to death for our trespasses and raised for our justification' (Romans 4:24f.). Unlike the Synoptic gospels (which remain largely content to report and interpret events in the *life* of the preacher from Nazareth), Paul reflects on the significance of his Lord's *death* and *resurrection*.

Further, between Jesus and Paul the theme of God's rule dwindles in importance and dogmatic beliefs emerge. These trends also throw light upon an apparent shift of resurrection faith from the circumference to the centre of interest. Let me explain. Jesus preaches the demand of God's rule, not the truth of resurrection. God's kingdom is breaking into the world and calls for radical obedience. Men must undergo conversion. At the same time Jesus speaks and acts in such a way that a *future* authentication of his words, promises and actions is the presupposition of what he says and does. If God's rule challenges men here and now, it remains a reality which is yet to come. Only then can it be seen whether Jesus's promise expressed through such images as the Messianic banquet (Matthew 8:11) will be realised. In the Synoptic gospels clear affirmations that Jesus's stand would be vindicated through coming resurrection remain for the most part implicit, as do dogmatic beliefs about his person and function in general.

In Paul, however, dogmatic beliefs become explicit, ethical injunctions take second place and the theme of God's kingdom surfaces rarely. The apostle believes that with Jesus's death and resurrection the divine rule has begun. What Jesus preached as a coming reality has already been realised—in part, and provisionally—through the events of Good Friday and Easter Sunday. For Paul what lies ahead is the consummation of the world and entry through resurrection into the final kingdom. Occasionally Paul refers to this final divine rule to give weight to his ethical injunctions. 'Neither the immoral, nor idolaters, nor adulterers, nor homosexuals, nor thieves, nor the greedy, nor drunkards, nor revilers, nor robbers will inherit the kingdom of God' (I Corinthians 6:9f.). To sum up. Jesus preached an imminent kingdom and supposed a coming divine vindication of his message. Paul proclaims a resurrection already effected (that of Jesus) and a general resurrection still to come. If we attend to these changes between Jesus and Paul and the other data mentioned above, we can clarify the apparent unimportance of the resurrection at certain levels in the New Testament. This lack of attention *as such* does not throw doubt on the specific testimony for Christ's resurrection which we examined in I Corinthians and the gospels. We still need to confront squarely the value of that testimony.

## RESURRECTION AND EXALTATION

Closely allied to the problem of the uneven attention paid to the resurrection in the New Testament is the issue of the relationship between Christ's resurrection and exaltation. Did the notion that at his death Jesus was 'taken up' to God constitute the older model? Is it possible that the resurrection claim derived later from this prior scheme of exaltation? Could belief in Jesus's resurrection after all have been no more than a subsequent pictorial expression of an earlier and vaguer conviction that God had somehow exalted Jesus after the crucifixion?[1] If so, the resurrection claim made by Paul and the evangelist would seem to be fatally undermined.

To 'exalt' (*hypsoō*) means literally to raise on high or lift up, and figuratively to ennoble, place high in rank and power or enhance in position. Clearly this term and related expressions enjoy a broader area of meaning than the verbs for resurrection. Resurrection as the narrower term implies exaltation, but not vice versa. To be raised from the dead is necessarily to be exalted. But Elijah could be portrayed as being exalted without his dying and being raised from the dead (II Kings 2:1–13).[2] The two concepts diverge also inasmuch as resurrection includes a certain 'horizontal' element. Exaltation suggests simply a 'vertical' image: Christ is lifted from the world 'below' to heavenly glory 'above'. Resurrection first directs our attention 'backwards': the one who is raised must first have died. Only after this earlier event of death can he be raised either to resume in some fashion life on earth or to be taken up into heaven.

Was the more inclusive concept (exaltation) the primary one from which the claim about Christ's resurrection evolved? The

New Testament fails to support an affirmative answer. It seems that originally 'resurrection' and 'exaltation' were relatively independent interpretations of the same event. The resurrection claim was not derived from the less specific assertion that God had exalted Jesus in his death. This conclusion emerges, if we distinguish the following four patterns in New Testament accounts of Jesus's destiny:

1. Death is followed by resurrection (I Corinthians 15:3f.; Mark 9:31).
2. Death is followed by heavenly exaltation (Philippians 2:8ff.; Mark 14:62) or by 'entering into glory' (Luke 24:26).
3. Death is followed by (a) resurrection and (b) the effective continuation of resurrection in exaltation (Romans 8:34; Acts 2:32f.) or enthronement as Son of God and Messianic king of the last age (Romans 1:4).
4. Resurrection and exaltation are used interchangeably to describe what followed Jesus's death (Luke 24:26=24:46). (This seems true of Matthew 28:16ff., where Christ appears *both* as risen from the dead *and* as the exalted one who has been given all power in heaven and on earth.)

If we examine these and further examples, we fail to find that death-exaltation texts occur *early* in the New Testament, while the pattern of death-resurrection (or death-resurrection-exaltation) surfaces only *later*. In fact, if a pattern does exist, it is rather the opposite. The theme of 'exaltation' emerges as a comment on and subsequent interpretation of the resurrection. The death-resurrection model (along with the death-resurrection-exaltation model) appears in such earlier works as I Corinthians and Romans, and that in passages where Paul draws on traditional credal formulations. The earliest examples of the death-exaltation pattern come in Mark and in what is probably one of Paul's last letters, Philippians (where in 2:8ff. he quotes a hymn to Christ). It is highly unusual for Paul to pass over the resurrection and link the cross immediately with exaltation.

John, of course, writing towards the end of the first century, develops the theme of exaltation. The Son of Man who descends from heaven through the incarnation ascends back to the Father by way of being 'lifted up' on the cross. The crucifixion is both a physical raising up and the divine exaltation of Christ (3:14;

6 :62; 8 :28; 12 :32f.). The model has ceased to be *death leading to exaltation.* John speaks of a death which *is* Christ's exaltation and passage to the Father. At the same time the fourth evangelist does not dispense with the pattern of death-resurrection-exaltation (through ascension). When Christ meets Mary Magdalene he is portrayed as already risen but still on his way to the Father (20 : 17). When he eventually speaks to the disciples, he does so from the far side of exaltation (20 : 19ff.). John has good reason for not portraying Jesus as ascending into heaven at the moment of his death on the cross. That would lead directly to the docetic position that only the spirit ascends into heaven, while the body is left behind on the cross. Such an ascension of Jesus's spirit would run counter to John's affirmation that 'the word became flesh' (1 : 14). Perhaps John's view can be best stated as follows. The exaltation implied by Jesus being lifted up on the cross is manifested by the reality of the resurrection and ascension.

The author of Hebrews goes even further than John in using the concept of exaltation. The Christ of Hebrews is the Son of man who by obedient suffering mounts as pioneer to heavenly places and is installed there as priest. In that letter the only clear reference to the resurrection occurs in 13 : 20.

However we interpret the details of the exaltation theology found in John and Hebrews, evidence is lacking to show that an original conviction about Christ's exaltation in death came first, and only later this vague belief crystallised into the specific claim that he had been raised from the dead. We may not evade in that way the basic task of examining the credibility of the testimony offered by Paul and the evangelists. Did certain individuals and groups in fact encounter Jesus alive after his death? Did Mary Magdalene (and possibly other women) discover his tomb to be empty on the third day?

Before closing this discussion on exaltation, we should note the value of the image. It implies that the resurrection was no return to earthly life and transcended any mere resuscitation of a corpse. The same point, as we shall see, emerges not only from Paul's account of Jesus's resurrection but also from that offered by Luke and John. Finally, the image of exaltation is closely related to that of ascension. In a later chapter we can examine the place of Christ's ascension, specifically as found in Luke-Acts.

[1] Lloyd Geering argues this case in a recent book. 'At the very beginning' the Easter faith 'was not expressed explicitly in terms of resurrection, but in terms of the divine exaltation of the crucified Jesus.' This exaltation later came to be proclaimed as resurrection (*Resurrection: A Symbol of Hope* (London, 1971), p. 148; cf. pp. 146ff.).

[2] Geering recognises some distinction between (1) exaltation and (2) resurrection as an exaltation which includes victory over death (*ibid.*, p. 156). He fails, however, to explore the full scope of this distinction, which affects any parallel between the fate of an Elijah and that of Jesus.

# PART TWO

## *Faith*

# 5

# *The Resurrection and the Historian*

THE FIRST PART of this book formed an attempt to map carefully the essential New Testament evidence bearing on the resurrection. Without question, those chapters raised issues and took positions on matters of faith and theology. It is simply not feasible to ask 'purely historical' questions, while completely sidestepping evaluation of truth, issues of belief and matters of interpretation. Nevertheless, it seemed worthwhile trying first to get things straight about the New Testament testimony and adopt some provisional positions on the basis of evidence. My aim was to create a basis for discussing explicitly man's personal appropriation of the Easter message. In this chapter I plan to raise issues concerned with *past* evidence and the role of the historian. The following chapter will concentrate rather on the subjective pole of *present* experience and decision.

## THE HISTORICAL FRINGE

At first glance it may seem unnecessary to argue that the investigation of Christ's resurrection involves the historian. After all he has the right and duty both to investigate the records of all alleged happenings of the past and to pronounce upon the probability or otherwise that they did in fact occur. However, a little reflection may weaken our conviction about the historian's role. If we invite him to examine some episode, we would normally presuppose certain requirements as fulfilled: (1) that the sequence of events be somehow *observable* by ordinary physical means; (2) that the (empirical) *causality* be detectable; (3) that the thing itself be to some extent *intrinsically intelligible*; (4) that it offer some *analogy* to other events in history.

Let us look at these requirements in turn. The murder of President Kennedy can serve to illustrate the first requirement. There was a definite sequence of events leading up to those moments when Lee Harvey Oswald fired the fatal shots. In principle these events were observable by normal means. In fact various witnesses observed nearly all of the events which gave the assassin his target in Dallas on November 22, 1963. As regards (2), we will be reluctant to accept as factual that for which we can give no causal explanation. The report that several Roman graves were unearthed in a remote part of Texas will meet with disbelief, because we are unable to explain how they came to be there. Such alleged happenings (burials by ancient Romans) would remain incredible, so long as no one could detect how any Romans visited North America to leave behind them these tombs. Requirement (4) forms a comment on requirement (3). If some new event proves intrinsically intelligible, it does so because it yields comparisons to those events we already know. We can subsume it under some general law(s) of which it provides a new instance. Of course, every historical event remains unique, in the sense that it has neither happened before nor will happen again with all the same characteristics. There will be only one assassination of John F. Kennedy. Yet this event exhibited features in common with other such tragic murders of political leaders; there were some relevant analogies.

When we apply our four requirements to Christ's resurrection, we should be discouraged from continuing to raise historical questions. With respect to (1), the New Testament hardly suggests that the resurrection itself could have been observable by ordinary physical means. Even if witnesses had been present to see it happening, would there have been anything to observe? Matthew has an angel appearing to open the grave in front of pagan witnesses (the Roman guards) and Christian women. But he stops well short of attempting to describe Christ's resurrection or alleging that someone could have witnessed the event itself (28:1–4). As Paul explains in Galatians (1:12, 16), he learned of the resurrection subsequently through special divine revelation—certainly not the historian's normal access to information. Our difficulty here touches both the resurrection itself and the appearances of the risen Christ. Most New Testament scholars would be reluctant to assert that the risen Christ became present in such a way that neutral (or even hostile) spectators could have observed him in an ordinary 'physical' fashion. If Annas or Pilate had kept company after the crucifixion with Peter and the other disciples, they would most likely have seen nothing at all when Christ appeared.

Requirement (2) can be met only in the most general terms. The New Testament nowhere advances beyond the simple claim that divine causality effected the resurrection. As regards requirement (3), Christ's return from the dead transcends our understanding. The New Testament accounts remain content with vague comparisons: this event resembled someone 'standing up' or 'being woken from the sleep'. Finally, the resurrection evades comparison with other events in history. According to the New Testament, this event differs from *all* events in the (empirical) history of the world. A fully new, professedly unique happening, it constitutes the beginning of the end of universal history. Christ's resurrection represents for the early Christians much more than the return of one dead man to life. Here death is definitively overcome in an event which must be compared with the creation of the world (Romans 4 : 17, 25).

Moreover, we risk turning the historian into a theologian, if we ask him to include the resurrection among the proper object of his study. He deals normally with events that have human and other natural causes. We ought to have serious misgivings about requiring an historian to recognise and integrate into his explanations alleged 'special' interventions *in history*, whether merely providential or miraculous. At most he may be expected to record and offer some elucidation of the fact that the Babylonian captivity, the fall of Jerusalem in A.D. 70 and other biblical events were acknowledged by certain people as 'acts of God'. It is not the historian's duty to verify (or refute?) the claim that God 'deeply' engaged himself in these events and so disclosed in a special way his intentions. The resurrection lies much more outside the proper sphere of historical studies, and that for two reasons. The New Testament both (1) expounds this event as the transit of the dead Jesus *out of history* to a glorified life in the 'other' world of God, and (2) attributes it to divine causality *alone*. Unlike the fall of Jerusalem where Titus and the Roman soldiers played their role, the resurrection was *ex hypothesi* effected only by God.

Whether we accept their testimony or not, it should be clear that Paul and the evangelists do not represent the resurrection as an inner-historical event, the mere resuscitation of a corpse which then resumes life under ordinary bodily conditions. Jesus moves to a transformed state of full and final existence so that he no longer belongs to history in a normal spatio-temporal sense. He leaves the ordinary limitations of bodily life to enjoy a 'glorious' (Philippians 3:21), 'pneumatic' existence, freed from the possibility of decline and death (I Corinthians 15:43ff.). It makes no historical sense to ask *where* (in a proper localisable sense) the risen Jesus was to be found one year after his resurrection. We lack the spatio-temporal data necessary, for example, to undertake a biography of the risen Christ. Since the New Testament asserts such a transit to an existence outside normal historical conditions, it seems that either to affirm or to deny the truth of this alleged resurrection is not *as such* to make an historical judgment.[1]

Nevertheless, it would be wrong to repudiate all involvement of the historian in our assessment of Christ's resurrection. The allegation that women discovered the tomb to be empty obviously remains open to ordinary historical investigation. Likewise, the historian can examine the testimony of that particular group of men who claimed Easter appearances at a particular time in a particular country. He may discuss the possibility of their being hallucinated at the time, as well as the results of this experience in their later lives. He can dispose of theories about their having created the whole story on the basis of some myth about a dying and rising God.

Finally, the historian can mark off the alleged resurrection in terms of ordinary time. Granted that the actual resurrection was a creative action of God on the crucified and buried Jesus of Nazareth, nevertheless, it was alleged to have happened at a particular time. At one time men did not say, 'God has raised Jesus from the dead'. At a subsequent time they said just that. There exists an historical 'fringe' to the resurrection which calls for the historian's attention, even if he rightly refuses to take the event itself as an object for his direct study.

By speaking of 'fringe' questions, I do not wish to rule out *a priori* the possibility that the historian could disprove the resurrection. Given appropriate evidence, he might establish that the women visited the wrong grave, that grave-robbers stole the body, that the apostles perpetrated a deliberate fraud, or even that Jesus was not executed under Pontius Pilate at all. Without the crucifixion there would have been no resurrection. While the resurrection may not be open to positive proof by the historian, he could in principle demonstrate that certain presuppositions (for example, that Jesus lived and died) or attendant claims (for example, that his grave was discovered to be empty) were false. In brief, if the historian cannot verify the resurrection, he could in principle disprove it.

Hence it is not open to us to claim that the resurrection has nothing at all to do with historical enquiry. Easter faith does not prove totally immune to historical judgments, as if it belonged to a special, religious sphere.

### PERSONAL INVOLVEMENT

In any case we would succumb to an illusion, if we characterised as disengaged and (in principle) non-religious the historian's work in examining the 'fringe' questions. Neither here nor elsewhere should historical study be pressed into the mould of (some supposedly neutral) natural science. Since Wilhelm Dilthey we have been forced to recognise that in the sphere of man there are no 'pure facts', no 'scientific' history. It is only as something human, meaningful and conditioned by personal attitudes that history becomes present. In any case, as Michael Polanyi and others have argued, even scientific knowledge, whether in the social sciences or in the natural sciences, far from being totally 'objective', forms a tissue of personal priorities, appropriations and interpretations.

Hence we may not postulate the fiction of some neutral starting-point for the historian in his investigation of the questions surrounding Christ's resurrection. He will examine the evidence as one who either accepts the resurrection or rejects it, or else perhaps as one who lacks a firm position through being as yet substantially unacquainted with the New Testament claim. He will undertake his work with certain antecedent convictions about God. He may, for instance, restrict the scope of God's intervention by presupposing empirical observation as the standard which determines the possibilities for new events. As resurrections from the dead clearly do not form part of the reality which we ordinarily observe, these will be ruled out *a priori*. A Canadian historian once told me that he found Jesus's alleged resurrection an embarrassing part of Christian faith. As dead men do not rise, the resurrection could only have been a quaint way of expressing hope two thousand years ago. My friend's world-view ('dead men do not rise') dictated the conclusions he was prepared to draw from the Easter-texts of the New Testament. The real issue for him concerned the possibility of God raising dead men to life rather than the specific issue of Jesus's resurrection. At every level the personal convictions of historians condition their hypotheses, conclusions and even views of the so-called 'facts themselves'.

What role then do personal convictions and commitment play in accepting the Easter proclamation? What contribution is made by the evidence both for the historical 'fringe' of the resurrection and for other matters of the past? These questions must be faced in the following chapter.

[1] Although not precisely for his reasons, I agree with Lloyd Geering that we should remove Jesus's resurrection 'from the class of events which are properly called historical and which are open to historical investigation'. *As such* it 'lies outside the scope of historical enquiry'. Geering, however, goes on to remark that whereas the Creeds (which affirm the resurrection) 'commence with the words, "I believe . . .", this is not the way an historian commences his book' (*Resurrection*, p. 216f.). Certainly it would be an unusual historian who began his work with a statement of faith. Nevertheless, the personal beliefs of historians deeply condition both their account of the 'facts' and their interpretations of them. We ignore the 'creeds' of historians at our peril.

# 6

# *Accepting the Resurrection*

We might decide that the truth or falsity of the Easter message can only be settled by investigating the evidence in the most unprejudiced manner possible. In approaching this task we will recognise the illusion of attempting a totally 'scientific' enquiry and—conscious of our own prior convictions—will try our best to prevent interference from these subjective dispositions in assessing the case for and against the resurrection. Is such an objective approach arguable and feasible? Do we rightly approach the issue by simply asking such questions as: Can we rationally account for the given evidence by some alternative hypothesis? Or does this evidence from the past by itself constrain us to accept the resurrection as having truly taken place?

Among contemporary apologists for the resurrection Wolfhart Pannenberg pre-eminently insists that the only way to deal with the issue is through an impartial investigation and objective assessment of the evidence.[1] However, he also acknowledges that men could be discouraged from accepting the case for the resurrection by their failure to appreciate what risen life could mean. Hence he explores the existential striving and questioning which can give credibility to the assertion of life for the whole man beyond death.[2] He willingly concedes a great deal of truth to the view that arguments for Christ's resurrection find a sympathetic hearing only from those who appreciate the meaningfulness of the resurrection for themselves. Not even Pannenberg supposes that the mere scrutiny of evidence from the past clears up the issue of Easter faith.

It seems to me that acceptance of the resurrection involves both evidence from the past and present personal experience. 'My' decision of faith now can not substitute for a rational examination of the Easter reports derived ultimately from the apostolic witnesses. Conversely, such an examination does not call for a wrong-headed attempt to suppress subjective dispositions as sources of unfortunate interference. In this chapter I plan to discuss first the role of evidence and then the place of personal commitment in accepting the Easter message.

### WHICH EVIDENCE?

In the debates about the resurrection apologists have divided with respect to the evidence which they considered most decisive. Some have pointed to the emergence and progress of the Christian Church as facts which remain unexplained (or even inexplicable) unless we accept Christ's resurrection. This argument may highlight the difficulty of accounting otherwise for the spectacular rise of the Church despite Jesus's ignominious crucifixion. Thus Alan Richardson maintains: 'The *real evidence* for the resurrection of Jesus is the existence of the Christian Church at all, if we have regard to the circumstances in which the earthly life of Jesus had apparently ended in such crushing failure and disappointment.' The force of the argument lies in an appeal to causality: 'Every effect must have a cause sufficient to produce it.' 'The unique effect' in question is the rise of the Christian Church. This effect can not be attributed to Jesus's life which ended so disastrously. In the circumstances the only cause sufficient to have set the Church going was his resurrection.[3]

C. F. D. Moule offers a somewhat different and, to my mind, a more penetrating version of this argument. He looks for some cause which not only was 'strong enough' to launch the Church in the first instance, but also proved 'tenacious enough to keep up their [sc. the Christians'] distinctiveness over against the pious Judaism to which they otherwise belonged'. Ultimately this cause was not some new ethic or anything less than the true conviction that God had raised Jesus from the dead.

> There was nothing to discriminate Christians initially from any other Jews of their day except their convictions about Jesus, and it was these which kept them from lapsing back into

> Judaism, or, rather, which ultimately forced them out of Judaism; which means either that these convictions were justified, or else, if they were not, that the rise and continuance of the Christian Church still await explanation. As an historical phenomenon, the coming into existence of the sect of the Nazarenes cannot be explained (it seems to me) by anything except its distinctive features; and these are due, if not to a huge reality, then to deliberate lying, or to misapprehension; and neither of these latter circumstances seems adequately to account for the facts.[4]

Richardson and Moule point to serious evidential considerations. Not only the origin of the Christian Church (despite Jesus's execution) but also the distinctiveness of this new religion over against Judaism call for explanation. Both these arguments would, of course, have lacked force in the first decade or so of Christianity. In those days there was little or no proof that Christianity would prove tenacious enough to maintain its distinctiveness over against pious Judiasm. The rise of the Christian Church had not yet proved a striking enough phenomenon to call for some sufficiently striking cause. Moreover, the first Christians nominate the cause in question, Jesus's resurrection. Some of them claim to have seen him alive after his death. In evaluating the truth of their assertions, the success of their message and other considerations may play a supplementary role. But ultimately we must scrutinise the credibility of their testimony itself.

## THE LIMITS OF THE EVIDENCE

The correct starting-point for assessing the evidence must be I Corinthians 15. Paul sets great store by the fact that he can appeal to a consensus. The leading teachers in the Christian community agree on this testimony to the Easter encounters, whatever differences of opinion may exist about other matters. Paul's desire to name as many resurrection witnesses as possible leads him to list even the appearance to James! (I Corinthians 15:7.) (The Jerusalem Church led by James threatened to impose the observance of the Jewish law upon gentile Christians—a threat which provoked Paul's violent reaction; see Galatians 2:1ff. and 11ff.) In offering this common testimony, Paul neither argues from some allegedly neutral stand-point nor attempts to prove

Christ's resurrection to interested but as yet uncommitted enquirers. He is reminding the Corinthians of what they already accept. The same point probably holds good for the Easter stories in all the gospels. It is unlikely that any of the gospels intend to present testimony to interested but uncommitted readers, who do not yet accept Jesus's resurrection and believe the Christian message.

When one examines the accounts both of the resurrection appearances and of the discovery of the empty tomb, what degree of probability or certainty does this testimony deserve? How credible are the apostolic attestations? First, this evidence leaves unexplained the inner nature of the resurrection. With the 'how' of the alleged event left vague, the 'that' becomes more questionable. Second, the evidence derives from men who lived nearly two thousand years ago and belonged to a culture markedly different from our twentieth-century advanced industrial societies. This temporal and cultural gap can affect credibility of their story. Third, the evidence in question is presented by a limited number of friends. Jesus appeared only to a restricted number of persons over a relatively short period of time. In Paul's exceptional case the experience of seeing the risen Lord subdued the unbelief of an enemy. On the basis of Acts 22 : 9 and 26 : 13f., we might be tempted to classify Paul's companions as neutral witnesses. While sharing the vision of light, they failed to hear the voice; only Paul understood the words of the risen Christ. (According to Acts 9 : 7, they heard the voice, but saw no one.) Essentially they did not participate in the encounter. It is the testimony of insiders alone which constitutes the evidence. In Acts 10 : 40f. Luke shows that he is aware of the objection that only believers come forward to testify to Christ's resurrection: 'God raised him on the third day and made him manifest: not to all the people but to us who were chosen by God as witnesses.' No (impartial?) non-Christians are available as witnesses for the risen Christ's appearances but only deeply committed believers.

Later the Greek philosopher Celsus held up to ridicule the fact that the risen Jesus revealed himself only to his followers, and failed to appear either to his opponents or his judge. The non-canonical Gospel of Peter and Gospel to the Hebrews also betrayed obvious sensitivity on this point by adding neutral and even hostile witnesses to the resurrection.[5] In a naive, fantastic drama the Gospel of Peter not only described the resurrection, but attempted to make both pagan guards and Jewish elders witnesses to the event.

> Now in the night in which the Lord's day dawned, when the soldiers, two by two in every watch, were keeping guard, there rang out a loud voice in heaven, and they saw the heavens opened and the two men come down from there in a great brightness and drawn nigh to the sepulchre. That stone which had been laid against the entrance to the sepulchre started of itself to roll and gave way to the side, and the sepulchre was opened, and both the young men entered in. When now those soldiers saw this, they awakened the centurion and the elders —for they also were there to assist at the watch. And whilst they were relating what they had seen, they saw again three men come out from the sepulchre, and two of them sustaining the other, and a cross following them, and the heads of the two reaching to heaven, but that of him who was led of them by the hand overpassing the heavens.[6]

Matthew had prepared the ground for such an approach by adjusting the Easter narrative to include some testimony from outsiders. In front of the Roman guards an angel descends from heaven to roll away the stone and announce the resurrection to the two women who had come to look at the grave. Even though these guards at the sight of the angel 'tremble' and 'become like dead men', nevertheless, some of them are able to report to the chief priest, 'all that had taken place' (28 : 1ff.). Events immediately related to the resurrection (the removal of the stone and the angelic proclamation) become public facts, observable to outsiders.

Yet need we be so anxious to find evidence from outsiders? Must we discount evidence which remains unsupported by neutral or hostile spectators? Obviously not. The testimony of 'insiders', if interpreted judiciously, can count as evidence. The absence of neutral witnesses is no automatic reason for rejecting testimony.

A determined sceptic like David Hume indicates that the status (and number) of available witnesses does not constitute his real objection. *No evidence* would be sufficient to establish the resurrection to his satisfaction. Let me put the point this way. Even if someone were raised from the dead, God could never provide enough proof to convince Hume that the event had truly taken place. In his famous example Hume supposes that in 1600 Queen Elizabeth I died, was buried, after a month appeared alive, resumed the throne and governed England for three more years before dying again. He would refuse to accept that 'so signal a violation of the laws of nature' had taken place and would attribute to 'the knavery and folly of men' this story, even though attested to by the Queen's contemporaries and accepted by 'all the historians who treat of England'. Hume's rejection of the evidence for Christ's resurrection is clear.[7]

Hume reminds us that we should—and normally do—require more evidence before accepting extraordinary claims than commonplace ones. What he fails to appreciate is that belief in Christ's resurrection transcends the mere acceptance of some amazing event 'out there' and 'back there' in history. His example about the return of Elizabeth I from the grave ignores this point. The personal implications for 'me' of Christ's resurrection are enormous. This event affects deeply the way we construe human life and the kind of policies we adopt.

Faced with the issue of the evidence for Christ's resurrection, some scholars like Pannenberg emphasise the role of historical reason. The evidence, although limited, remains reliable and suffices for a rational acceptance of the resurrection. Others like Marxsen press the claims of present commitment. Even if we could establish through evidence that Jesus rose from the dead, this hardly touches the heart of the matter. New life can happen for me now, if I accept Jesus's message.

> We are given the chance of making, after all, the venture of faith. That means, quite simply, not trying to be self-sufficient but letting go. We are offered the chance of seeing through the circumscription of our lives and throwing it aside. We are offered the chance of letting tomorrow's worries belong to tomorrow and not to today. We are offered the chance—a chance which is also a challenge—of seeking out the other person instead of defending ourselves from him. I do not now need to say who offers us all this. *He* comes today and offers us what I have called the cause of Jesus . . . I take the risk of

> doing what he asks, contrary to all human reason. In the course of so doing I experience the fact: it is true . . . Suddenly you take the risk again, contrary to all reason—and then again, and yet again. And one day you discover that you are on the path through *this* life *to* life.[8]

Both solutions prove less than successful. Pannenberg rightly points out that present commitment fails to provide an independent source of information about the past. Faith cannot settle the fact that Paul really encountered the risen Christ.[9] Yet by exalting the role of historical reason and maintaining that faith depends upon prior knowledge, Pannenberg ends up by doubling the problem of certainty. We must first establish through reason the certainty that the resurrection took place. Then a firm faith can be built on this historically verified conclusion. But what if we finish up with no more than historical probability? What is added to give faith its certainty? Marxsen's position may appear a welcome relief in the face of many problems about the interpretation of the Easter texts. Oppressed by a cloud of words from the exegetes, we could welcome a liberating 'leap' from the ambiguities of debate to the moral purity of generous self-engagement. I do not wish to discredit the good features of this option, but it should be clear that the fundamental cognitive problem will not be solved in this manner. Men rightly continue to ask: What happened to Jesus himself after his death?

### THE EXPERIENTIAL CORRELATE

Ultimately an assent to the reality of Jesus's resurrection combines knowledge of past facts with an interpretation of present experience. The information provided about the past offers a credible report. Yet in expressing belief in the resurrection—or rather in Jesus as risen from the dead—we are going beyond the evidence. In a true sense we cannot wait until all the evidence is in. We do not know, for example, how many people will continue to accept the reality of the resurrection, nor what course the Christian community that was set going by an enthusiastic Easter faith will take. But as actors in the world now we must choose and stake ourselves on an attitude vis-à-vis the resurrection. This issue directly concerns practice as well as theory. What kind of life will be possible on the basis of belief in the resurrection? Will this belief enable us to deal creatively and productively with the world? We cannot properly understand what is being asserted by the message of the resurrection, if it remains alien to us and we do not face action on this basis. The question which a girl vehemently put to me once at the end of a lecture must be answered: 'What the hell does the resurrection have to do with life anyway?'

In brief, an experiential correlate is needed. To say that God raised Jesus will prove unintelligible and unacceptable, unless our own lives yield some knowledge of God and allow us to experience now something of the resurrection. A resurrection that is simply affirmed and remains totally invisible will be at best suspect. We need to translate it into statements which concern our human existence now. What questions does the resurrection answer for us? How can the risen Jesus come alive for us? In what sense does he rescue us from our bewilderments and satisfy our needs? Personal experience does not substitute for a reasonable scrutiny of the reports from the past. Rather it constitutes the context in which those reports can be understood and appropriated.

This experiential correlate will vary from person to person. No one ought to imagine that we can come up with some standard list of experiences or fixed set of questions and answers. Each of us takes in a somewhat different world and then, prodded by our needs, desires and evaluations, does 'our own thing'. It would be false to surrender to some abstractions or abridgments which simplified many different and distinct human attitudes into a few, easily available alternatives. Yet it is also true that some generalisations can be risked. Four words ('death', 'expectation', 'meaning', and 'hope') gather together much of what can be said.

My first generalisation is a negative one. Only those who have experienced death in some form can know what resurrection means. Loved ones may die. Episodes of sorrow, guilt, tragedy or separation may occur which seem far worse than physical death itself. Not only individuals but also racial and religious groups and even whole nations know only too often inhuman oppression, fearful social and political convulsions, systematic terror and catastrophic defeat in war. When human beings are 'raised' from such deadly episodes, their situation can allow them to discern what it means to say that Jesus was raised from the dead. The apostolic testimony to the resurrection will then be heard in a personal context of life after death, joy after sorrow, freedom after slavery, forgiveness after guilt, safety after terrifying danger, reunion after separation or whatever other form this reversal takes.

Our appreciation of the resurrection message may be rooted in a sense of the discrepancy which exists between what we *expect* as valuable for ourselves and what we actually *experience.* After events characterised by unhappiness, deprivation of personal freedom and failure, we can meet positive, if partial, experiences of happiness, freedom and success. Can we retain, repeat and above all enlarge these experiences? How can demonic negativity be effectively and definitively excluded? This quest for wholeness both illuminates and facilitates belief in Christ's victory over death. Faith in his resurrection entails expectations of our final happiness, complete success and ultimate freedom to be found with him.

Perhaps this point would be put more forcefully in terms of man's search for *meaning*—meaning both about himself and about his world. Wherever we discover sense and meaning in the world, the more we are enabled to understand ourselves. Let me specify three areas of experienced meaning which yield partial answers to the question: What would the new order of Christ's resurrection look like? First, man has engaged himself more and more in the attempt to create and shape his world. He investigates the laws and powers of nature in order to effect a more valuable and meaningful order. Despite pollution and other failures, we see human creativity engaging itself at every level to humanise nature. Second, concern for freedom, the spread of co-responsibility and the desire for greater human solidarity constitute widely held ideals, even though effective practice may still be lamentably restricted. Mankind exhibits a widespread yearning for justice, freedom and the dignity of shared responsibility. Third, most men experience meaning at its most intense in their personal relationships to family and friends. Here I am recognised in love by others and receive the freedom to be truly myself. Both in actual life and through the medium of literature, art, films and the theatre we experience mutual love as valuable and meaningful. Let us take these three areas of experienced meaning and try to project for ourselves a totally humanised world where full justice and freedom hold sway in a universe of mutual love. Such a projection can yield some sense for an Easter faith. Insight into a truly meaningful future through designating such possibilities could facilitate belief in Christ's resurrection and its promise. To accept the Easter testimony is to accept the meaningfulness of human life as a whole.[10]

Finally, reference to human hope may yield some insight here. Acceptance of Christ's resurrection proves feasible only when linked with hope for one's own resurrection. If a man gives up hope, he gives up himself and simultaneously the possibility of assent to the Easter message. We cannot make such an assent without also answering what Camus identified as 'the only real philosophical question', that of suicide. Clearly, if less dramatically, Kant's third question at the end of his *Critique of Pure Reason* ('What may I hope for?') suggests that the truth or falsity of the resurrection message will be decided only with reference to 'my' destiny. Belief in Christ's past resurrection emerges by challenging 'me' to revise my forecasts and forebodings of the future. This belief entails the conviction that 'my world' is headed towards fulfilment, not mere ending or catastrophe.

## FREEDOM OF FAITH

Finally, the element of free decision affects man's acceptance of the resurrection. The disciples on the Emmaus road must be willing to adopt a new perspective on the scriptures before they can recognise Christ (Luke 24:13–32). John seems to suggest that something more than a mere physical movement is involved, when he portrays Mary Magdalene as 'turning around' (20:14) before she can acknowledge the risen Lord. Matthew also implies that a meeting with the resurrected Jesus presupposes that men are willing to encounter him; they remain free not to do so (28:17).

This freedom does not, as we have maintained, exclude evidence, as though the resurrection were a transcendent happening which should lead men to disdain grounds for faith. The resurrection transcends history, and yet is no purely suprahistorical or extra-historical event. It touches history through the encounters with Christ as well as through the discovery of the empty tomb. What is not properly datable and localisable leaves evidential traces within history. Despite his anxiety to safeguard faith's freedom, Paul considers it his responsibility to remind the Corinthian Christians of reasons for accepting the resurrection. Evidence need not endanger the freedom of faith.

Nevertheless, insistence on evidence risks encouraging the distorted view that assesses the resurrection simply as an episode which is supposed to have happened back there and back then. Christian faith, however, exists only in the link between the subject and the object, between the believing self and the risen Christ to whom allegiance is given. His resurrection took place independently of us. Yet it remains a reality which we know by dwelling in it. We will accept the apostolic testimony to the resurrection only when we acknowledge the risen Lord speaking to us now : 'I *am* the resurrection and the life.'

Easter faith is not based simply on our knowledge of reliable past testimony to the resurrection, as if it were a mere prolongation of this historical knowledge. Faith may not exist independently of historical knowledge, but it can not be reduced to it. Witnesses report the event of Christ's resurrection, an event which demands of us a new commitment of faith. This demand will make sense or fail to make sense within the context of 'my' world. Human experiences are endlessly different and distinct. There is no question of some standard experiential context in which the apostolic testimony to Christ's resurrection will be heard. While this testimony sounds real and convincing to one man, it may sound absurd and illogical to another.

[1] *Jesus—God and Man*, p. 99.

[2] *Ibid.*, pp. 83ff.; *What is Man?*, tr. D. A. Priebe (London and Philadelphia, 1970), pp. 41–53.

[3] *The Gospel and Modern Thought* (London, 1950), pp. 55, 57; italics mine.

[4] *The Phenomenon of the New Testament* (London and Naperville, 1967), pp. 11, 19.

[5] For details see von Campenhausen, *Tradition and Life in the Church*, pp. 64f.

[6] 8:35–40; translation from *New Testament Apocrypha*, ed. W. Schneemelcher, I (Philadelphia, 1963), p. 185f.

[7] *An Inquiry Concerning Human Understanding*, ed. C. W. Hendel (New York, 1955), X, p. 138.

[8] *The Resurrection of Jesus of Nazareth*, p. 183f.; cf. pp. 149ff.

[9] *Jesus—God and Man*, p. 109.

[10] See Viktor Frankl's *Man's Search for Meaning* (London and Boston, 1962), where this distinguished psychiatrist describes his experiences in Auschwitz and other concentration camps. Even under the most inhuman conditions men can survive, if they find meaning strong enough to support their conviction that life is worth preserving.

# PART THREE

# *Theology*

# 7

# *The Gospels and Easter Theology*

UP TO THIS point we have been exploring issues concerned with (1) the factuality of Christ's resurrection and (2) man's acceptance of the Easter proclamation. Our initial aim was to clarify the original sense and historical origins of the Easter texts. We went on to investigate what is involved in accepting or rejecting the apostolic testimony to the resurrection. We now transfer our attention to matters of theological interpretation.

The first part of this book began with the testimony of I Corinthians 15 and then offered a critical discussion of the Easter story in the four gospels. Where that opening section moved from Paul to the evangelists, I find it desirable in this third part to move in the reverse direction. After dealing with some aspects of resurrection theology in the gospels and with the specific question of the empty tomb, I plan to end with reflections which largely centre on Paul's doctrine of the resurrection.

All the New Testament witnesses to the resurrection are manifestly affected by their faith in the risen Christ. They do not offer us 'purely factual' reports, even if such were possible. They would be the last writers in the world from whom to expect such reports. The evangelists provide rather an amalgam of believing witness and historical reminiscence with the aim of eliciting and developing the faith of their readers. In the resurrection stories all the evangelists wish to express theological perspectives and serve the needs of the early Church. Repeatedly we find them touching—often enough lightly—on such themes as the Eucharist, the forgiveness of sins, the missionary task of the Church and the interpretation of scripture. Let me draw attention to four of the most important topics of this Easter theology: revelation, the unique role of the apostolic witnesses, the 'realism' of Luke and John, and the image of the ascension.

## REVELATION

In the various resurrection stories the theme of revelation surfaces repeatedly. Divine help must be available before man can perceive God's supreme disclosure in Christ's resurrection. The angel in Mark's account functions to suggest that the truth conveyed lies beyond the reach of ordinary observation. The women can see the empty tomb where Jesus's body had been laid. But they need to hear the angelic word ('he has risen, he is not here'), if they are to grasp the revelation entailed (16:6). Matthew remarks that at the rendezvous on a mountain in Galilee the eleven disciples become aware of a presence. Some recognise (and worship) at once their risen Lord, while others remain irresolute and doubtful. Christ must come and speak, before they all know perfectly well who it is and what their mission is to be (28:16–20). On the sacred mountain of revelation the risen Lord commissions his Church to preach, baptise and teach.

Matthew and Mark direct our attention somewhat to the past. Their explicit (but not total) concern is to answer the question: What happened in the days following Jesus's crucifixion? While not ignoring past events, Luke and John show a more obvious interest in the continuous (revelatory) experience of the risen Lord. This manifestation occurs above all in the liturgy. Repeatedly the Easter texts of Luke and John imply that he is to be encountered in (1) the Eucharist, (2) meal fellowship, (3) the forgiveness of sins, (4) the reading and explanation of scripture, (5) the dynamic operation of the Holy Spirit and (6) simply in the experience of faith. The two evangelists point to these elements of Christian life which signal Christ's continual and effective presence in his Church. Let me offer examples of such theological reflection in Luke and John.

(1) In 'the breaking of the bread' the two disciples at Emmaus find their eyes opened and they know their risen Lord (Luke 24:30f., 35). The Eucharistic overtones are unmistakable. The Christians of the late first century, Luke implies, will realise

Christ's presence when they meet for their Eucharist. (2) Closely allied with such times are those manifestations of the Lord when the community gathers for meals and/or worship. He reveals himself as they gather in his name (Luke 24:33ff.; John 20:19ff.). At breakfast together on the lakeside the disciples 'knew it was the Lord' (John 21:12f.).

(3) John explicitly connects the forgiveness of sins with the presence of the risen Christ (20:23). He suggests this connection in other ways as well. Something more than a mere physical movement seems implied, when John portrays Mary Magdalene as 'turning around' (20:14) before she can recognise the risen Christ. The discernment that brings Easter faith involves conversion. This holds true of the 'third time that Jesus was revealed to the disciples after he was raised from the dead' (John 21:14). Peter's meeting with the risen Christ becomes the occasion of forgiveness for the apostle who had denied his master. At several points in his narrative John transmits to his readers his conviction: 'Where you experience the forgiveness of sins, there you can know the risen Christ to be present.'

(4) Luke clearly links this presence with the revelation mediated through scripture. The disciples on the Emmaus road are offered and accept a new perspective on the biblical witness as they come to acknowledge Christ's presence (24:13–32). The risen Christ enables his followers to perceive how the scriptures testify to him as the one who must suffer and enter into glory (Luke 24:44ff.). (5) John and Luke obviously point to the operation of the Holy Spirit as manifesting the effective presence of the risen Lord. Where the Spirit and his gifts are received, there the risen Christ is at work. (6) Finally, John implies that where men confess Christ as 'Lord and God', there Christ—invisibly—meets them. Hence the fourth evangelist concludes without a farewell scene or a narrative account of an ascension, and leaves Jesus's last words ringing in his readers' ears: 'Blessed are those who have not seen and yet believe' (20:29).

Thus in various ways the Lucan and Johannine Easter narratives draw their readers' attention to the lasting and manifest presence of the risen Christ. For his part Matthew also alerts us to this presence through the promise, 'I am with you always, to the close of the age'. This is a presence mediated through the world-wide mission, the administration of baptism and the instruction which recapitulates Jesus's commandments (28:19f.).

### UNIQUE WITNESSES

By drawing attention to the lasting experience of the risen Christ within the Christian community, Luke and John seem to call into question the unique role attributed to the resurrection witnesses. Was the experience of the risen Christ enjoyed by Peter and the other disciples in the days following the crucifixion really of an essentially different kind from later encounters? Does Luke imply that any Christians may enjoy an Emmaus-road meeting by knowing their Lord in the reading of the scriptures and the 'breaking of the bread'? Should we acknowledge a democracy of access to the risen Christ, so that all post-resurrection generations would be on an equal footing with respect to the possibility of experiencing his presence? Louis Evely confidently answers in the affirmative: 'The apparitions of which the Apostles speak are apparitions that we ourselves can experience.'[1]

Luke and John, however, respond otherwise. Despite—or rather along with—their concern to link the official witnesses with other Christians, these two evangelists clearly interpret the post-Easter encounters of these witnesses as different in principle from experiences of the risen Lord which later Christians might enjoy. Luke represents Christ as ascending into heaven after having spent some time with the core group of his disciples. The events of the forty days (in which the risen Lord met, spoke and ate with that privileged group) differed fundamentally from all later encounters. As reported in Acts, not even Paul's Damascus-road meeting was on a par with the Emmaus-road episode. John also carefully discriminates other Christians from those disciples to whom the risen Christ appeared. Thomas came to belief when he saw the Lord. His road to faith differed from that of later Christians who 'have not seen and yet believe'. The official witnesses to the resurrection did not enjoy some privileged form of faith. But they played a unique role in testifying to the 'signs', so that others also might 'believe that Jesus is the Christ, the Son of God' (John 20:29–31). Writing at the end of the first century, John invites those 'who have not seen' to believe in reliance on eye-witness testimony.

Three steps are involved here. In raising him from the dead,

God acts on Christ who then acts on the apostolic witnesses by appearing to them. In their turn they transmit the message to others by carrying through their missionary task of proclaiming the resurrection. These stages emerge in the speech which Luke attributes to Paul in Acts 13: 'God raised him [sc. Jesus] from the dead; and for many days he appeared to those who came up with him from Galilee to Jerusalem, who are now his witnesses to the people' (verses 30–32). In John's gospel we have, of course, reached the point where the resurrection is no longer regarded as God's (or the Father's) exclusive act, but is described as Jesus's own doing. 'I lay down my life,' Jesus declares, 'that I may take it again. No one takes it from me, but I lay it down of my own accord. I have power to lay it down, and I have power to take it again' (10:17f.). Yet in John also the risen Christ acts on a restricted set of witnesses in terms similar to the pattern Luke offers. Peter and the other disciples receive from the risen Lord their mission to mankind. For this they are endowed with the Holy Spirit and empowered to forgive sins (John 20:21–23). They enjoy an experience of the risen Christ and will play a role which differentiates them from later hearers and readers of the Christian message, the 'you' which the fourth gospel addresses (20:31).

These witnesses to whom the risen Christ appears can also be called the founding fathers of the Church. Their unparalleled link with the resurrection goes hand in hand with their unique task of bringing into existence the Christian community. Among the witnesses Peter receives special attention. We find a hint of this pre-eminence in Mark where the angel instructs the women: 'Go, tell his disciples and Peter that he is going before you to Galilee; there you will see him' (16:7). In the Marcan Easter narrative the story reaches its climax not with the discovery of the empty tomb nor with the angelic announcement of the resurrection, but with the instruction to communicate the message to 'his disciples and Peter'. Only Peter is singled out for mention by name.

Paul's list of resurrection witnesses places first Christ's appearance to Peter: 'He appeared to Cephas, then to the twelve' (I Corinthians 15:5). Luke echoes this priority of Peter as Easter witness in what looks like an early item of tradition embedded in the Emmaus story: 'The Lord has risen indeed, and has appeared to Simon' (24 : 34). Peter's testimony brings about Easter-faith in 'the eleven' and 'those who were with them' (24 : 33). Later appearances function to confirm this faith rather than to create it for the first time. The appearance to Peter is not only chronologically first but also constitutive for the faith of others. Luke has prepared his readers for this by Jesus's remark at the Last Supper that when Simon Peter had 'come to himself', he would 'lend strength' to his brothers (22 : 31f.). The primary appearance to Peter serves Luke's purposes by explaining the apostle's prominence in Acts 1–12. In this way Luke can bridge the gap between Jesus's ministry and the history of the early Church in which Peter serves as leader.

John's gospel also reflects Peter's status as primary witness to the resurrection. After her discovery of the opened tomb Mary Magdalene runs to tell 'Simon Peter and the other disciple, the one whom Jesus loved'. They both then visit and inspect the empty grave (20 : 1–10). The appendix to John (Chapter 21) manifestly maximises both the role of Peter as resurrection witness and the pastoral function conferred on him by the risen Christ. Peter leads the fishing expedition which results in the meeting with the Lord on the lakeside and the command, 'Feed my lambs, feed my sheep'. In both chapters twenty and twenty-one we find some modifications attached to the early conviction that Peter is the primary Easter witness. The specific 'Johannine' testimony receives some degree of priority. In the race to the tomb the 'beloved disciple' both outruns Peter and comes to faith when he enters the tomb and 'sees'. Perhaps the reader is meant to understand that Peter also finds faith at the sight of the empty tomb, but this is not stated. It looks as if the fourth gospel wants to represent the beloved disciple as first to believe. Chapter twenty-one qualifies Peter's prominence as Easter witness in several ways. If Peter wades ashore to meet the risen Christ, it is the beloved disciple who first recognises the stranger on the shore. The same disciple outlives Peter to guarantee the Easter testimony at the end of the apostolic age (21 : 18ff.). At the same time, however, Peter's role as primary Easter witness remains substantially unchallenged in chapter twenty-one. A further hint of deference towards this role may occur when the beloved disciple waits for Peter before entering the empty tomb (20 : 3ff.).

Further, the primary appearance to Peter has left its trace in

Matthew's account of Peter's confession at Caesarea Philippi (16:13–20). Favoured by revelation ('flesh and blood has not revealed this to you'), Peter receives 'the keys of the kingdom' from his risen Lord. As a consequence of this revelation and his commission he proceeds to found the Church. This narrative is at least shaped by Peter's role as first resurrection witness, even if we may not with certainty characterise it as an Easter episode retrojected into the period of the ministry.

Finally, Simon may have first obtained the name 'Cephas' (=Peter) on the basis of the earliest Easter appearance. This privileged episode created or at least strengthened his function as 'rock' among the first disciples. He gathered about him the scattered disciples to bring into being the Christian community. The risen Christ's subsequent appearances to groups and individuals confirmed and legitimated what had already been effected through Peter. In parenthesis let me suggest that the position of the Bishop of Rome would be most helpfully understood as that of successor to Peter in his role as the first Easter witness. Such an approach avoids any suggestion of private privileges, subordinates the Pope to the risen Christ and suggests well the task of one who in the strength of his Easter faith gathers the scattered community. It is a pity that other Petrine texts from the New Testament are inscribed high on the walls of St. Peter's Basilica in Rome but not those words from Luke, 'The Lord has risen indeed, and has appeared to Simon'.

### REALISM IN LUKE AND JOHN

A further obvious (and troubling) feature in at least two of the gospels is their realistic approach to the resurrection. In their Easter accounts Luke and John are obviously at pains to establish the indubitable physical reality of the risen Christ. Whereas in Matthew the risen Lord merely speaks,[2] in Luke he walks a road for several hours, sits at table, invites others to handle him and eats fish to convince his disciples that he is no ghost (24:15ff., 41–43). 'See', he says, 'my hands and my feet, that it is I myself; handle me, and see; for a spirit has not flesh and bones as you see that I have' (24:39). In John he shows his disciples his hands and side, and invites them to touch his risen body in which the marks of his wounds still remain (20:20–27). This forms a startling contrast to the rest of the gospel. So often

Jesus seems like a divine, majestic visitor who does not belong to man's normal material world. Likewise the cruel realism of the passion is played down. In the resurrection, however, John presents Christ at his most corporeal by introducing graphic, physical details. Why do Luke and John go out of their way to express in vivid, natural details the corporeal reality of the risen Christ? Perhaps they wish to counter Gnostic and Docetic views which 'spiritualise' the resurrection. Luke may also plan to stress the physical reality of the resurrection because he knows the kind of difficulties Greek (pagan?) readers would have with this belief (cf. Acts 17:32). The Lucan and Johannine realism contrasts strikingly with Paul's reflections in I Corinthians 15. Here we detect no suggestion that Jesus returns to any earthly kind of existence and activities. Raised and exalted to heaven, he emerges from his invisible state to encounter momentarily certain privileged witnesses. His body is no longer 'physical' but 'spiritual'. 'Flesh and blood cannot inherit the kingdom of God' (I Corinthians 15:44, 50). In brief, Paul's notion of transformation through resurrection challenges the picture of physical reanimation that the third and fourth gospels offer.

John and Luke seem, however, to realise that their 'realistic' emphasis could create the impression that Christ's resurrection amounted to nothing more than the resuscitation of a corpse. To check such a misunderstanding they convey the other-worldliness and transformation of his risen body by portraying Christ as passing through closed doors (John 20:19, 26) and as suddenly appearing and disappearing (Luke 24:31–36). The new condition of the risen Lord allows Luke to represent him as disappearing by rising into heaven (perhaps 24:51; certainly Acts 1:9). A need to do justice to the 'otherness' of the risen Christ is implied also by another recurrent motif in Luke and John. People who had known the earthly Jesus fail, at least initially, to identify the risen Lord. In the Emmaus episode the two disciples recognise Jesus only in the moment of his disappearance (Luke 24:31). Mary Magdalene takes him to be a gardener (John 20:14f.). Peter and the other disciples out fishing do not at once identify the stranger who calls to them from the beach (John 21:4ff.). In a low key both Luke and John call our attention to the transformation involved in Christ's resurrection. If they emphasise his *physical* presence to counter 'spiritualising' aberrations, they also allow for a certain 'heavenly otherness' to prevent crassly materialistic views which would reduce the resurrection to the reanimation of a corpse.

The Jerusalem tradition of Luke and John 20 (and the Galilee tradition of John 21) also stress the identity of the risen Christ with the earthly Jesus. On his side, the Easter encounters are moments when he identifies himself with an 'It is I myself' (Luke 24:39), or expressly links what he now says in his risen state with what he has said during his ministry (Luke 24:44). On the disciples' side, the moment when they acknowledge the risen Lord as none other than the Jesus whom they had known constitutes a climax in these encounters (Luke 24:31; John 20:16; 21:7, 12).

This theme of identification is not wholly lacking in the Galilee tradition of the Synoptic evangelists. Matthew remarks that at the rendezvous in Galilee the disciples become aware of a presence. Some recognise at once their risen Lord, while others remain doubtful. Christ must come and speak before they all realise perfectly well that this is Jesus whom they had known. If he now sends them to 'make disciples of all nations', the mission relates back to his historical existence. They are to teach the observance of all that he has already 'commanded' during his ministry. The Lord who now speaks to them is the same Lord who had often spoken to them. If we correctly interpret the account of Peter's confession at Caesarea Philippi as a resurrection story retrojected into the ministry of Jesus, Matthew offers a further startling case of the identification theme. The Lord who encounters Peter at Easter is none other than the Jesus of the gospel story. The evangelist feels perfectly free to switch the context of the story from post-Easter existence to the pre-Easter existence of Jesus. Finally, in a muted fashion Mark too exemplifies this identification theme. He deliberately relates the encounter with the risen Christ in Galilee ('there you will see him, *as he told you*' (16:7)) to a promise which Jesus makes on his way to Gethsemane: 'After I am raised up, I will go before you to Galilee' (14:28).

### THE ASCENSION

Lastly, we come to the issue of Christ's so-called 'ascension'. Such passages as Romans 10:9 show that at an earlier stage in the New Testament period the resurrection remains undifferentiated from any 'subsequent' exaltation and/or ascension: 'If you confess with your lips that Jesus is Lord and believe in your heart that God raised him from the dead, you will be saved.' In I Corinthians 15:4ff. the risen Christ is understood to appear 'from heaven'. He does not first return from the grave to an interim existence on earth from which he ascends into heaven. Luke, however, describes just such a separate ascension of the risen Christ: 'As they were looking on, he was lifted up, and a cloud took him out of their sight. And while they were gazing into heaven as he went, behold, two men stood by them in white robes, and said, "Men of Galilee, why do you stand looking into heaven? This Jesus who was taken from you into heaven, will come in the same way as you saw him go into heaven" ' (Acts 1:9–11).[3]

Luke has not derived this theme of ascension from Mark or any other identifiable source. When we examine Paul and pre-Pauline traditions (like I Corinthians 15:3b–5 and Romans 1:3b–4), we find no ascension separated from a prior resurrection. Why then does Luke introduce and depict in physical terms an ascension into heavenly glory? His willingness to describe the ascension contrasts strangely with the fact that like the other evangelists (and Paul) he remains silent about the hidden, mysterious act of God in raising Jesus from the dead. An additional puzzle arises from the ending of Luke's gospel where 24:50f. reads: 'Then he led them out as far as Bethany, and lifting up his hands he blessed them. While he blessed them, he parted from them.' Some texts add: 'And was carried up into heaven,' but the shorter reading seems to be the original. But whether one reads the longer text and speaks of an ascension( or more strictly an assumption) or the shorter text and speaks of a parting, nevertheless, the ascension or parting takes place on the resurrection day itself.[4] What then of the forty days which separate resurrection and ascension in Acts 1:3?

First things first. Seemingly, Luke feels no contradiction either between the one day of appearances in his gospel and the forty days of Acts 1:3, or between an ascension on Easter day and one forty days later. He does not intend to give an exact date for the ascension. If he once mentions 'forty days', later in Acts he speaks vaguely of an ascension after 'many days' (13:31) or simply omits any temporal indications (10:41). Commentators have frequently pointed out that the round number of forty enjoys significant biblical and Jewish parallels. Moses remained on Mt. Sinai for forty days and forty nights with the Lord (Exodus 34:28). Elijah travelled forty days and forty nights to Horeb, the mountain of God (I Kings 19:8). After his baptism Jesus himself was forty days in the desert (Mark 1:13). But do earlier parallels explain all? Hardly. Luke seems more concerned to link Easter and Pentecost than to introduce decorative parallels. Like Paul and John he appreciates the intimate association between the risen Christ and the Holy Spirit. His 'forty days' helps to ensure that his readers will understand Pentecost as the extension of Easter and the manifest outpouring of the Holy Spirit as the gift of the risen Christ.

The question still has to be asked: What do we make of the ascension itself? Within the framework of Luke's theology the ascension serves several purposes. It *closes* the series of regular resurrection appearances, whether to individuals or to the groups of disciples. Paul's later Damascus-road encounter is, in Luke's view, of a different order. Second, Luke acknowledges that the end of the world will be delayed, so that the gift of the Holy Spirit does not herald an imminent *eschaton*. Rather Pentecost inaugurates the universal mission of the Church. Faced with a delayed *parousia*, Luke offers this pastoral message to his contemporaries: 'Play your role in the mission with confidence in the power of the Spirit.' Third, in Luke 24 the departing Christ imparts his priestly blessing to his disciples who respond with worship and prayer. The farewell scene forms a glorious climax to the story of his earthly ministry. Yet this scene should not suggest that Christ has gone away on a kind of extended sabbatical leave to wait somewhere for the day of his return. Rather the Church's world mission will take place under his invisible, yet real presence. Occasionally, as at Paul's Damascus-road encounter, that presence discloses itself in a startling fashion. Fourthly, the ascension story, especially in Acts, testifies further to what we have noted above, Luke's desire to maintain the indubitable physical reality of the risen Christ. The spectators witness Christ being carried up and away. Once again the evangelist wishes to affirm the corporeality of Christ risen and ascended.

Finally, careful observation shows that the ascension fits a key Lucan theme, continuity in salvation history. The one who ascends remains identical with the one who has already preached, suffered, died and been raised. The witnesses who had accompanied Jesus from Galilee to Jerusalem (and could testify to his death and resurrection) also see him ascending. These are the 'men of Galilee'—as Luke significantly calls them (Acts 1 :11)—who can guarantee the continuity between the one who departs and the one who has preached in their home land. The journey up to Jerusalem, that important Lucan motif which begins at 9 :51, forms the first stage of ascension : 'As the time approached when he was to be *taken up to heaven*, he set his face resolutely towards Jerusalem.'[5] The going to the holy city is at the same time a going up to heaven. With the ascension comes the climax of that pilgrimage from Galilee to suffering, death and resurrection in Jerusalem.[6]

This chapter has struggled with some important topics in the resurrection theology of the gospels—revelation, the role of the apostolic witnesses, the 'realism' of Luke and John, and Luke's ascension theology. We have chewed over and picked apart ideas which perhaps were not always clearly formulated by the evangelists themselves. That holds true of the theme held over till the next chapter, the theological implications of the empty tomb. Can we pin down and spell out the significance of something to which all four evangelists testify, the discovery on the third day that Christ's grave was empty ?

[1] *The Gospels Without Myth*, p. 165.

[2] A. George comments helpfully: 'Matthew does not delay over the bodily condition of Jesus. He admits, in fact, that he is recognisable to the witness of his earthly life (28:17) . . . He does not have Luke's specifications on the reality of his body, nor on his "appearance". Undoubtedly the reason for this must lie in the fact that Matthew is a Jew writing for Jews: neither he nor his readers could conceive the Risen Jesus as not having a very real body' (*The Resurrection and Modern Biblical Thought*, ed. P. de Surgy (New York, 1970), p. 61).

[3] An ascension (as distinct from the resurrection) is found sporadically elsewhere in the New Testament: see John 20:17; Ephesians 4:8–10; I Timothy 3:16; Hebrews 4:14; 6:19; 9:24; I Peter 3:22.

[4] The fourth gospel, the only other gospel to allude to an ascension, likewise fits it into the resurrection day (John 20:17).

[5] Cf. Acts 1:11, 22.

[6] For a fuller discussion of the ascension in Luke see R. H. Fuller, *The Formation of the Resurrection Narratives*, pp. 120ff.

# 8

# *The Empty Tomb in Theological Perspective*

IN AN EARLIER chapter we sought an answer to the question: Was Jesus's tomb in fact found to be empty on the third day? There it was argued that Mark's story of women making this discovery should be accepted as substantially reliable.

Such a position is frequently challenged in two ways. Some dismiss the discovery story as a *secondary* development from the earlier preaching of the resurrection. Thus Peter Hodgson writes: 'The empty-tomb traditions are not to be judged as historical reports but as later interpretations of the belief that Jesus was risen and at work in the world.'[1] (In passing one might ask: Does Hodgson imply that 'historical reports' and 'interpretations' are mutually exclusive?) Gordon Kaufman suggests that the 'story of the empty tomb' 'may have been relatively late in appearing—an extrapolation from, and objectification in physicalist terms of, the original reports of appearances'.[2] The story of the empty tomb can be challenged on these and similar *historical* grounds.

But there are also those writers who frankly dismiss this story for reasons of *theology* and—equivalently—faith. Evely finds the story both irrelevant for faith and theologically questionable. He describes his own position as follows: 'For me personally, it makes little difference whether Christ's tomb was empty or not. I would have exactly the same faith in his resurrection in either case.' In a theological vein he questions: 'If . . . the resurrection of Christ is our resurrection, why should we expect his to take place in a way different from ours?'' This query recalls the case which G. W. H. Lampe develops from 'the truth of the incarnation'. In stronger tones than Evely he insists that Christ's resurrection 'cannot be of a different order' from our resurrection. By becoming man Christ entered fully into that human condition which entails physical corruption after death. Hence his body *must* have decayed in the grave.[4] *Pace* Lampe, one may reasonably wonder whether a theology oriented to the incarnation necessarily demands the conclusion that Jesus's body could not have been raised in a transfiguring resurrection. We can return to this issue later in the chapter.

Finally, some scholars raise *both* historical *and* theological objections to the story of the empty tomb. Hans Grass, for instance, contends that (1) faith is directed towards the person of the risen Christ, (2) God did not need an empty tomb, and (3) in any case the Easter faith of Peter and the other disciples arose when they encountered the risen Christ, not when they found the tomb to be open and empty.

> God did not have to make the tomb empty in order to effect his Easter miracle . . . The Easter faith arose far from the burial place and independently of it. The historical reality of the empty tomb is no item by which the resurrection stands or falls . . . We do not believe in the empty grave, but in the risen Lord.[5]

Points (1) and (2) are theological, point (3) historical.

In an earlier chapter I maintained the historical case for the tradition of the empty tomb. Such argumentation could be endlessly prolonged. It does not, for example, necessarily count against the historical truth of this tradition that it first appears in Mark (probably in the mid-sixties). We cannot simply assert that what is recorded later derives—by way of unhistorical extrapolation and interpretation—from reports about another matter (the appearances of the risen Christ), which happen to be written down earlier (in I Corinthians 15:5–8). I suspect, however, that the real problems with the empty tomb are theological, not historical. Unless these theological problems are allowed to come into the open, I feel like an elephant fighting a whale, unable to make effective contact with my opponents. Hence this chapter aims (1) to offer some insight into the role played by the empty tomb in a full resurrection faith, and (2) to point the way towards clearing up difficulties which Lampe, Grass and others raise. The next chapter can also contribute some help, inasmuch as it explores that identity-in-transformation which Paul ascribes to the risen body.

## NEW TESTAMENT RESERVATIONS

The New Testament warns us against an anxious preoccupation with the empty tomb which would run a clear risk of exaggerating its value. In Mark 16:1–8 the three women who find the grave open and empty must hear the resurrection message ('He has risen, he is not here') before they come to believe. The resurrection is asserted ('He has risen') before the body's absence is noted ('See, here is the place where they laid him'). The explanation of resurrection is not 'deduced' from the physical fact of an empty tomb. The angel does not answer some such question from the women as, 'What has happened to the body?' The angel reveals the unexpected—the resurrection—and so brings them to faith. Mark has no particular apologetic for the empty tomb, nor does he assign it any independent kerygmatic status. The message which the women are to carry back is not 'Come and see Jesus's empty tomb', but 'He is going before you to Galilee; there you will see him'. Luke explains that the women's message meets with incredulity: 'These words seemed to them [sc. the apostles] an idle tale, and they did not believe them' (24:11). The report of the empty tomb and vision of angels proves insufficient to bring others to faith.

In John, however, the empty tomb has gained enough importance that it may suffice to establish faith for those perfectly disposed to believe. It has become a Johannine sign, a means of grasping an other-wordly truth. Neither the appearances nor any angelic message are required before the beloved disciple, a model of the authentic believer, comes to faith (20:8). As a type of those who believe without seeing the risen Christ, he stands in sharp contrast with doubting Thomas, who makes faith dependent upon physical contact with the risen Christ. Readers are meant to value the faith of the beloved disciple, precisely because he has not yet understood the predictions of scripture that Christ must rise from the dead (20:8f.). Even so, he believes.

Nevertheless, the fourth evangelist acknowledges that the sheer fact of an empty grave remains ambiguous (20:2, 13–15). He puts into the mouth of a believer the objection of unbelievers that unidentified grave robbers had provided the basis for the Easter faith. Mary Magdalene states this view: 'They have taken the Lord out of the tomb, and we do not know where they have laid him.' (A similar explanation appears also in Matthew where the chief priests and elders allege that Jesus's disciples stole the body.) John, however, seemingly wishes to give the lie to the polemical statement that the tomb was robbed. He observes that the grave-clothes remained neatly in the tomb—something that would not have happened if thieves had been at work. 'Simon Peter came . . . and went into the tomb; he saw the linen cloths lying, and the napkin, which had been on his head, not lying with the linen cloths but rolled up in a place by itself' (20 : 6f.).[6]

To sum up. The New Testament authors maintain the fact of the empty tomb but freely admit its ambiguity. What theological value then could the empty tomb enjoy? What part should it play in Easter faith? Will we be left in the odd position that we might accept the fact of the empty tomb but fail to integrate it into our understanding of the resurrection? Or is it even out of the question to effect such an integration?

## A SIGN

We can usefully initiate a theological answer by noting that for the New Testament writers the empty tomb did not constitute a proof of some reality but a sign. They were interested not so much in answering the question, 'Was the tomb empty?', as in pointing to the *significance* of the fact that it was empty. This empty grave meant much more to them than, so to speak, a return from the tomb. It stood for a return from the dead and all that was implied by that. A man's burial signified that he was removed from the land of the living. He had fallen into the power of death; the earth or the stone which covered his body separated him from the living. To be in the grave was to be in the under-world (Psalm 49 : 14f.; Luke 16 : 22f.). Hence Christ's resurrection as a victory over death (I Corinthians 15 : 54–57) was understood to have loosed the bonds of death and deprived death of its power (Acts 2 : 24). Christ now possessed the keys of the underworld (Revelation 1 : 18), so that he could guarantee that the forces of death would not prevail against the Church (Matthew 16 : 18).

To maintain that the empty tomb stands as a sign of Christ's victory over death does not take us very far. After all such a victory could assume many forms. The real theological value of this doctrine lies elsewhere. The empty tomb acts as a safeguard against 'spiritual', docetic, Platonising interpretations which expound the resurrection as an escape from 'here' to 'there'. In such explanations the real world lies elsewhere. By his death and resurrection Jesus leaves this illusory world of decay behind him. He entered our human situation but eventually gives it up completely as irredeemably hopeless. His body can only be abandoned to the corruption of the grave. Those who dispense with an empty tomb can readily end up asserting what looks scarcely distinguishable from the immortality of Jesus's soul. Thus Lampe may explicitly refuse to introduce such a doctrine into his discussion of the resurrection.[7] But he erodes this position seriously when he speaks of 'we' and 'our personalities' continuing to exist, although not 'in the mode of physical being'. He even admits: 'If my relationship to God continues, then I must continue: as my self, or my soul (I take these terms as synonymous), not in this present bodily mode of existence, but living because the God on whom my life depends will maintain his grace towards me.'[8] In these terms the victory of the resurrection becomes a continued existence outside 'the mode of physical being' of Jesus's 'personality'.

It has become conventional to remark that a dualistic anthropology is no longer self-evident. Modern man has ceased to believe in an immortal soul inhabiting his body. I wonder. Platonism may be hardier than we suspect. Perhaps it is in the nature of things that there should always be attempts to interpret the resurrection as some survival of Jesus's 'inner' self which makes a break with his old bodily existence. A transformed body which promises a transformed world presents imaginative difficulties which are almost too much to take. It is easier—either overtly or covertly—to deal with an immortal soul and deck out the long-standing Platonic model with new plausibility. One of my former students, George Hunsinger, expressed this trend as follows. For those who believe in such immortality the hope is that time will be left behind, not redeemed; that death will be surpassed, not destroyed; that evil will be eluded, not defeated. In this scheme God allows the believer to transcend the old creation through an immortality to be enjoyed beyond the grave in 'another world'.

Acknowledgment of the empty tomb guards us from the constant temptation to let our interpretation of Christ become docetic. Too easily we can play down the bodily reality of the risen Christ, portray the resurrection as some kind of liberation of a 'spiritual' Christ and treat the physical world as illusory and incapable (or at least unworthy) of salvation. It is hardly a coincidence that Rudolf Bultmann's demythologised view of the resurrection both omits the empty tomb and goes hand in hand with an existentialist theology which fails to do justice to man's physical and social nature.[9]

For a proper appreciation and appraisal of the empty tomb it is important to hold two complementary affirmations before our attention. This doctrine asserts something about God as Redeemer, as well as something about our material world. On the one hand, God intends to save the whole man and the world. He begins to transform the world and redeem human history by raising up Jesus's dead body. On the other hand, the world is neither an illusion from which we must awake nor an evil which will prove irredeemable. God shows this by beginning his work of re-creation in favour of Jesus's crucified body. The past can be recovered as raw material for the future kingdom. As we shall argue, there is an identity-in-transformation between the earthly and the risen Jesus.

Let us come back now to the theological objections against the empty tomb raised by Lampe and Grass. Lampe starts from the truth of the incarnation: 'That the Word of God was truly made man is the heart of the gospel. God incarnate entered our condition.'[10] From this central truth, as we have seen, Lampe 'deduces' the conclusion that Christ's body *must* have decayed in the grave.

First things first. Paul for one would question the opening assertion that we should simply take the incarnation as 'the heart of the gospel'. For the apostle 'the heart of the gospel' is found elsewhere—in the saving death and resurrection of Christ. For these saving events the 'sending' of the pre-existent Son of God formed a prerequisite. In Pauline theology the incarnation as such does not redeem man. We may not assume some incarnation-oriented theology of John or the later Greek fathers to be indisputably the central point from which the other Christological mysteries must be interpreted. We come back to this issue in chapter ten.

Secondly, it remains a questionable procedure to 'deduce' a particular fact (about Jesus's bodily fate) from a principle, even the principle of the incarnation. At least since the Middle Ages Christology (and Mariology) have been disfigured by theologians' readiness to take general principles and derive—by some logical necessity which may no longer seem either logical or necessary—specific facts about such matters as the extent and nature of Jesus's knowledge. The principle involved in Lampe's argument leaves aside differences between Jesus and ourselves. But some differences—for instance, Jesus's sinlessness—remain, as Lampe allows. Many theologians have argued that it is precisely such differences which make it both appropriate and intelligible that Jesus's resurrection should differ from the resurrection which Christians hope for. His sinlessness militates against his enduring the whole of human destiny through undergoing bodily corruption in the grave. Yet here again any straightforward *deduction* of a particular fact (the empty tomb) from a principle should be rejected as a dubious procedure. At best the principle of sinlessness serves to illuminate further an already accepted belief in the empty tomb.

Finally, as one of my former students (Daniel Harrington) pointed out in an unpublished paper, even an incarnation-oriented theology need not lead to a rejection of the empty tomb. Lampe formulates the doctrine in this way: the Son of God has become *man*. My own formulation would reverse the emphasis: the *Son of God* has become man. While Lampe feels it imperative that Christ should fully share our fate, I would argue that his primary role is to elevate man and to summon him to that which lies beyond his powers. In other words, the redemptive goal of the incarnation needs to be respected. This goal can throw light on the empty tomb, or at least prevent us from misinterpreting the point of the incarnation as (more or less) sharing the human condition as such.

To conclude with some brief remarks about the position of Grass. We gain nothing by capitulating to his assertion that 'we do not believe in the empty grave, but in the risen Lord'. Such an antithesis remains foreign to the New Testament. To strike out the empty grave would be to tamper seriously with the Easter witness of the early Church. In examining that witness we concluded that essentially the empty-tomb story was an historically reliable, if subordinate, part of what the first Christians had to proclaim about Christ's resurrection. They announced the women's discovery on the third day, but did not propose this announcement as some alternative to belief in the risen Christ. Such belief had been first established by appearances to individuals and groups. The independent discovery of the empty tomb constituted a negative sign serving to confirm those appearances. Karl Barth rightly maintains that although 'Christians do not believe in the empty tomb but in the living Christ', this does not imply 'that we can believe in the living Christ without believing in the empty tomb'. For it forms 'an indispensable sign' which 'obviates all possible misunderstanding'. It precludes misinterpreting the existence of the risen Christ as something 'purely beyond or inward. It distinguishes the confession that Jesus Christ lives from a mere manner of speaking on the part of believers. It is the negative presupposition of the concrete objectivity of his being.'[11]

[1] *Jesus—Word and Presence* (Philadelphia, 1971), p. 236.

[2] *Systematic Theology: A Historicist Perspective* (New York, 1968), p. 419f.

[3] *The Gospels Without Myth*, p. 160.

[4] *The Resurrection*, pp. 59, 97, 99.

[5] *Ostergeschehen und Osterberichte*, p. 185.

[6] See further W. Reiser, 'The Case of the Tidy Tomb', *Heythrop Journal*, 14 (1973), pp. 47-57

[7] 'Easter . . . has nothing to do . . . with the idea that there is some part of our being that is inherently immortal: some entity that we might call a soul. No. As far as our human nature is concerned, when you're dead you're dead; and so was Jesus' (*The Resurrection*, p. 10).

[8] *Ibid.*, pp. 45, 60.

[9] For details see my *Man and His New Hopes* (New York, 1969), pp. 31ff., 58ff. In responding to his critics Bultmann significantly remarked: 'The chief aim of every genuine religion is to escape from the world' (*Kerygma and Myth*, p. 113).

[10] *The Resurrection*, p. 92.

[11] CD III/2, p. 453; IV/1, p. 341.

# POSTSCRIPT TO CHAPTER 8

Lloyd Geering's *Resurrection: A Symbol of Hope* offers a further recent example of historical reasons being advanced against the truth of the empty-tomb story, whereas the real motivation lies elsewhere. Deeply held theological and philosophical convictions appear dominant. Let us look first at some of the historical and literary arguments which manifestly fail to carry the weight of his thesis.

Geering remarks about 'the key persons' in 'the tomb story' (Mark 15:40–16:8), Joseph of Arimathea, Mary Magdalene, Mary the mother of James and Salome, that they 'appear nowhere else in the whole Gospel'. He expresses further surprise that 'these persons are never heard of again; they find no mention in the early chapters of Acts, which is our only picture of the primitive church'. He concludes: 'One would have expected those who had discovered the empty tomb to have played a prominent part in the primitive church.'[1] 'Really? For various social and religious reasons (of which we need not approve) no women played such a prominent role in the primitive church. Why should we expect an exception to have been made in the case of those who discovered the empty tomb, when they would have been in competition with the twelve (who had closely associated with Jesus during his ministry) and the apostles (to whom the risen Christ had appeared)? The circle of apostles, of course, overlapped that of the twelve, but an apostle (for instance, Paul) need not be one of the twelve. Many have taken the very obscurity of the 'key persons' in the tomb story as a point in favour of its historicity. Joseph of Arimathea and the others were remembered simply for their generous intervention on that occasion. The story was not later fabricated and attributed to prominent figures like Peter and other members of the twelve who were known to have been around at the time.

Geering maintains that Mark 15 :40–16 :8 forms an (historically unreliable) appendix which was added later by the evangelist or another, and lacks *real connection with the body of the gospel.* He considers briefly one objection to this view, the fact that 16 :7 manifestly takes up 14 :28. However, he fails to discuss the careful way in which the evangelist prepares the way for Jesus's passion, death and *resurrection* through chapters 8, 9 and 10. The triple prediction that the Son of Man would suffer, be killed and *after three days rise again* forms no stray element in this section, but is carefully woven into teaching on the nature of Christian discipleship (8 :31; 9 :31; 10 :32–34). In view simply of these chapters it seems highly implausible that the evangelist could—even initially—have planned to conclude his gospel at 15 :39 without any reference to the resurrection.[2]

Geering attempts to deal with the argument of Von Campenhausen and others that if the story of the empty tomb were no more than a legend, it would not have specified three women who by Jewish law were not considered competent to testify. Against this Geering proposes three points: (1) 'The women are not being appealed to as witnesses to the resurrection in any case.' (2) 'In later gospels the empty-tomb story assumes an apologetic role in the proclamation of the Easter faith but that is not its function here.' (3) 'If the story had an historical foundation, and if the women had been regarded as witnesses to something vital, they would have found a place in the Pauline tradition.' As regards (1), the women are in a real, if not a strictly legal, sense introduced into the story as those who could testify to what they had found, an empty tomb. (2) Surely the absence of an apologetic role in Mark's empty-tomb story counts, if anything, in favour of the story's historical foundation. Strong apologetic motivation is not leading the evangelist to fabricate evidence or omit awkward details. (3) Paul's silence, as I have contended, provides no overwhelming reason for dismissing the story as unhistorical. It is not enough to argue that if it had been historical, Paul 'should have known about it no later than his conference with Peter and the other disciples'.[3] Paul may have known the story, but for good reasons decided not to introduce it in I Corinthians 15 :3ff.[4]

Beyond reasonable doubt Geering's real objection to the empty tomb rests not on dispassionately established historical conclusions but on theological and philosophical beliefs. He is sure that 'man, as a whole conscious being, does not survive death'. Hence what survived Jesus's death could only be the influence of his example and message: 'The death of Jesus did not bring to an end his power to attract men and to lead them to new life; on the contrary, because of his very death his power and influence have been experienced by men more fully and widely.'[5] An empty tomb would be unthinkable. The real issue with Geering transcends mere historical and literary arguments. His world view ('man, as a whole conscious being, does not survive death') dictates the conclusions he is prepared to draw from the Easter texts of the New Testament. In fact, the real point of debate with Geering concerns the possibility of God raising dead men to life. This Geering will not accept, seemingly because the assertion of such a possibility smacks of egoistic self-interest, whereas Jesus appealed for a 'readiness to empty oneself of all concern for oneself here or hereafter'.[6] Hope for resurrection must be ruled out as a morally objectionable, reward-oriented existence which proves incompatible with Jesus's call to selfless love. I can act properly only when I exclude such hope and remain content that my unselfish life will 'rise to a fresh mode of manifestation in the lives of men who follow'.[7]

Ultimately, the debate with Geering over the empty tomb leaves history far behind and brings up two theological issues: (1) Can God raise the dead? Is such resurrection compatible with or even 'demanded' by divine love? (2) Does unselfish love exclude hope for our own conscious, human future beyond death? Can we both love our neighbours as ourselves and hope that we will hear the invitation, 'Come, O blessed of my Father, inherit the kingdom prepared for you'? (Matthew 25:34.)

[1] *Resurrection*, p. 44f.
[2] *Ibid.*, pp. 48ff.
[3] *Ibid.*, pp. 55ff.; cf. pp. 35ff.
[4] See above, pp. 43-4.
[5] *Resurrection*, pp. 219, 228.
[6] *Ibid.*, p. 227.
[7] *Ibid.*, p. 232.

# 9
# *The Risen Life*

In the third part of this book we have transferred attention to the theological aspects and elaborations of Christ's resurrection. Undoubtedly, the most important contributor to such insights is the apostle Paul. Hence in these closing chapters we turn to examine major themes in Paul's theology of the resurrection. In the present chapter we begin to investigate the senses in which he gave his doctrine of resurrection a thoroughly Christological colouring. What did Paul have to say about the nature of that definitive life first enjoyed by the resurrected Christ and later to be lived by other resurrectees? But before we raise *theological* questions something must be said about the *historical* background to Paul's doctrine: the Jewish origins of his resurrection belief, the teaching of Jesus and the opposition against which Paul's teaching on resurrection was directed in I Corinthians. An appreciation of this historical background will throw light on Paul's theological understanding.

## ORIGINS

Paul, of course, did not invent belief in resurrection any more than Jesus himself did. Both men accepted a hope for resurrection as part of the religious tradition into which they were born. It was against a prior apocalyptic expectation of general resurrection that Paul interpreted Jesus's individual resurrection. But was Paul—and before him Jesus himself—'correct' in this belief? Or—to put the question another way—should our acceptance of resurrection stand or fall simply with the case of Jesus's resurrection itself? If so, it would not matter greatly how belief in resurrection arose or even that during his ministry Jesus showed that he expected a general resurrection (and perhaps his own prior resurrection). Let me state the issue in extreme terms. Can we afford to begin simply with Jesus's resurrection, examine Paul's reflections on it and flatly ignore prior Jewish beliefs? Such an 'isolationist' approach to Jesus's resurrection, however, seems just as intolerable as any other attempt to deal with Jesus himself without including his Jewish origins.[1] Moreover, as will be argued, the logic of Hebrew faith out of which resurrection belief grew suggests some illuminating comparisons with and contrasts to the kind of contemporary expectations considered above (in chapter six).

This resurrection belief may possibly have come from Persian religious thought into Judaism, where it was accepted by apocalyptic circles and the Pharisees. The extent of admitted Persian influence depends somewhat on our assessment of (1) the general effect of some basic Israelite beliefs about God and man, and (2) the specific role of prophecy in the development of apocalyptic. Let us take up these two points in turn.

Some ancient convictions in Israel yield a clue as to how the way was prepared for belief in life after death and, specifically, for acceptance of resurrection. On the one hand, the Israelites worshipped Yahweh as the God of *life*, the one who gave and restored life in its different forms to both individuals and the people. On the other hand, Yahweh was also a God of pre-eminent *justice*. Under Antiochus Epiphanes (died B.C. 164) a severe persecution began against those who lived according to the Mosaic law. Their just recompense could come only through life after death. If they had remained faithful to the divine covenant, was their annihilation possible? Without question, the martyrdoms in this Maccabean period were understood within the context of Israel's ancient faith and aided the development of resurrection belief. Those who clung to the faith of their fathers and died for their decision could confidently expect to be restored to life (II Maccabees 7). The evolution of faith in resurrection owed then a great deal to ancient convictions about Yahweh as God of life and justice—convictions which had already raised fearsome problems within the context of mere this-worldly expectations, as we see so often in the psalms, Job and elsewhere.

Furthermore, resurrection belief drew together aspirations for permanence which Israelites had expressed from their earliest times. In many memorable ways the Old Testament records yearnings for the continuous existence not only of 'merely' human blessings but also of life with God. Men yearned that somehow their own good name, their family, their tribe, their people and possession of the promised land should last forever. But they also cried out for permanence in their friendship with Yahweh. These various aspirations for continuity climaxed in that supreme assertion of human permanence, the belief that God would raise the dead.

Then the role of prophecy in the development of apocalyptic belief in resurrection must be mentioned.[2] We may not minimise the impact of prophetic passages like Ezekiel 37 (and perhaps Isaiah 53), which expressed hopes for the restoration to life of a whole people dead through sin. In that famous vision of the field of dead bones Ezekiel announced the renewal of the nation. The command of Yahweh could call back to life the bleached and dried-up bones. 'Thus says the Lord God: Behold I will open your graves, and raise you from your graves, O my people; and I will bring you home into the land of Israel' (37:12). The 'little apocalypse' of Isaiah (24–27) proclaimed in similar tones the restoration of Israel after its decimation by exile. From these expectations of national survival it was a short step to hopes for personal resurrection. Such a process could have been rendered all the more possible by divisions in the Jewish community. Israel as such no longer seemed an obvious religious unity. Along with the loss of vibrant self-consciousness as a people went a corresponding spread of individualism. Identity on a community basis waned. If a sense of the individual's worth was abroad, greater isolation also threatened him. It has been said that the emerging Roman empire would prove the first place in the world where a man could feel totally 'lost'.

So much for the origins of that late Jewish belief in resurrection which was taken up in the New Testament. These brief reflections should challenge the common and frequently unexamined supposition that 'resurrection faith is a late and rather erratic and marginal adjunct to biblical faith. While its formulation in terms of the individual was indeed a latecomer, it should be clear that it is, in a real sense, a logical outcome of Hebrew faith in God.'[3] That should not imply, however, that hope for resurrection loses some authority through being, at least in origin, not specifically Christian and possibly even having its roots in ancient Persian ideas which came to be admitted into Judaism. It would be silly to judge those Christian doctrines second-rate which originated in the Old Testament. Likewise, beliefs in Judaism should not be undervalued wherever they apparently fail to derive from some dramatic moment of divine revelation, but may have developed through reflection and contact with the religious ideas of non-Israelites.

In passing, let me stress that an examination of the origins for Jewish resurrection belief enjoys more than mere historical value as a background to the interpretation of Jesus and Paul. This enquiry ties in with the considerations offered above (in chapter six) on those human needs, wishes and hopes which can render the resurrection message credible. There are obvious correspondences between those Jewish convictions (which gave rise to hopes for a *coming* resurrection) and man's expectations now (which enable him to accept the apostolic message about Jesus's *past* resurrection). Nevertheless, at the risk of misrepresenting matters by over-simplification, we can contrast the considerations outlined in chapter six as man-centred—*anthropological*, if you like—with the strongly *theological* convictions which lay behind late Jewish faith in resurrection. This is not to take back what has been maintained about the historical context in which this belief surfaced—a context characterised by a heightened sense of the individual's worth as well as by deeper pessimism about the existing world order. But theological reasons were primary. The annihilation of the righteous individual appeared incompatible with divine fidelity and justice. In the faith of Israel belief in resurrection emerged as a corollary of theism. God would vindicate himself in the face of death and concomitant evils.

In the late Jewish period what calls for attention is the striking diversity between various resurrection doctrines. We find belief in the resurrection of righteous Israelites only (I Enoch 83–90), the resurrection for judgment of both righteous and unrighteous Israelites (I Enoch 6–36; II Baruch; probably Daniel 12:1–3), the resurrection of all just men—whether Israelite or non-

Israelite (probably II Maccabees), and the resurrection for judgment of all men (II Esdras). The last belief tallies with the kind of resurrection to either glory or punishment which we find in John 5:38. The Sadducees, of course, rejected all belief in resurrection. As a party they failed to survive the fall of Jerusalem. But prior to A.D. 70 their denial of resurrection might not have been nearly so insignificant in Jewish religious thought as we commonly imagine. Luke could mislead his readers with the suggestion that the whole Jewish race shared the Pharisaic hope for resurrection. He reports Paul as pleading before King Agrippa in the following terms: 'I have lived as a Pharisee. And now I stand here on trial for hope in the promise made by God to our fathers, to which *our twelve tribes* hope to attain, as they earnestly worship night and day. And for this hope I am accused by Jews, O king! Why is it thought incredible by any of you that God raises the dead?' (Acts 26:5–8).

Even within those circles which accepted life after death the situation remained fluid. Hope for life beyond the grave could be understood as involving (1) a reconstructed body, (2) a transfigured body, or (3) even no body at all. A very considerable divergence of opinion existed as to whether the resurrection body would be 'spiritual' or 'corporeal'. In II Baruch the just are described as being transformed into the splendour of angels (51:5). They will be changed into every form they desire—from beauty into loveliness and from light into the splendour of glory (51:10). On the other hand, a much more material view could be expounded. Some Jews assimilated the risen body to the earthly body. In another passage in II Baruch itself it is suggested that the earth shall restore the dead in the form in which it has received them (50:2). The replies of the seven brothers and their mother in II Maccabees envisage a reassembling of the limbs and straightforward restoration of the tortured bodies of the martyrs (7:14–38; cf. 14:46). Finally, in the book of Wisdom (which was probably written in the first century B.C.) the writer appears to have accepted the Greek doctrine of an immortal soul. He stresses the spiritual elements of the after-life and—to say the least—leaves unclear the fate of the body. Here we seem to meet belief in life after death involving no body at all.

The actual diversity in late Jewish attitudes towards the possibility and nature of resurrection makes nonsense of the monolithic view which Evely and others too easily suggest. Evely writes:

> *For a Jew of Christ's time,* a resurrection did not signify the reassumption of a body by 'its' soul; it signified instead the fact that man, in his totality, would know a life beyond this one, that what is essential in man would be eternalised. *For a Jew of that time*, however, the essential thing in a man was not his soul; it was to be an animated body—that is, a being indivisibly corporeal and spiritual.[4]

Certainly this account of man as an 'animated body' says much about current Jewish anthropological views. Evely echoes here, of course, H. W. Robinson's classic statement in *The People and the Book*: 'Man is an animated body, not an incarnated soul.' But future hopes for man were quite another matter. There was no such thing as 'the Jewish' view of resurrection.

### JESUS'S TEACHING

Jesus himself ran into the debate about resurrection when confronted with a comical objection excogitated to serve Sadducean casuistry.

> And Sadducees came to him, who say that there is no resurrection; and they asked him a question, saying, 'Teacher, Moses wrote for us that if a man's brother dies and leaves a wife, but leaves no child, the man must take the wife, and raise up children for his brother. There were seven brothers; the first took a wife, and when he died left no children; and the second took her, and died, leaving no children; and the third likewise; the seven left no children. Last of all the woman also died. In the resurrection whose wife will she be? For the seven had her as wife' (Mark 12:18–23).

In his reply Jesus based himself on 'the scriptures' and that 'power of God' which can transform human life into an otherworldly existence. He interpreted the new aeon by way of comparison not with this world but with the existence of 'angels in heaven'. The dead will rise, yet not so as to return to a this-worldly existence. Finally, in terms that find an echo in I

Corinthians 15 :34ff., Jesus flatly asserted that those who prided themselves on their knowledge of God were 'quite wrong'. They lacked insight into God and his plans for mankind. As the God of the living, Yahweh could guarantee man's continuing existence (Mark 12 :24–27).

Yet Jesus scarcely concerned himself with the question: What will the risen life be like? He clearly presupposed a future life (in heaven or hell), as well as specifically teaching that there would be a resurrection of the dead at the end. But what the Synoptic Gospels report him as saying about the risen life hardly takes us beyond the general assertion of an 'angelic', glorious state. He echoes Daniel 12 :3 to explain that 'the just will shine like the sun in the kingdom of their father' (Matthew 13 :43). He uses the stock image of the final Messianic banquet to indicate the joyful fellowship with God which belongs to the coming life of the just. If we wish to look for novelty in Jesus's teaching, we find it in his claims about his role in mediating future life as a unique agent of salvation and coming judge (Luke 12 :8; Matthew 25 :31ff., etc.). But for any possible elucidation on the nature of risen life we need to turn from Jesus to the apostle Paul.

## PAUL'S OPPONENTS

Paul's classic treatment of resurrection appears in I Corinthians 15. Nevertheless, many puzzles arise when we scrutinise this chapter in detail. What position(s) was Paul attempting to counter? What did his opponents actually hold? Intensive examination of the texts has led to no assured conclusions about the target(s) of his polemic. (1) It has been widely held that the opponents were Christians who shared dualistic, Platonising convictions about the next life, maintained the immortality of the soul, and flatly denied any resurrection of the body. (2) Other scholars have suggested that these Corinthian Christians had capitulated to that common scepticism about an after-life which drew mockery on Paul's proclamation of the resurrection (Acts 17 :32). They denied all hope for the next life. Hence they accepted Christianity as a this-worldly religion and no more. (3) According to a third view, Paul's opponents were 'enthusiasts', who believed that through baptism and the gifts of the Spirit they had already achieved resurrection. Like Hymenaeus and Philetus they 'swerved from the truth by holding that the resurrection is past already' (II Timothy 2:17f.). Proponents of this third view point to Paul's concern to check the Corinthians' self-satisfaction with their many spiritual gifts. This view finds support from passages like 4:8, but not from 15:19 and 15:32.

(4) Yet another interpretation can be maintained. Paul was arguing with people who believed in the transformation of those lucky enough to be still alive at the parousia, but refused to accept a general resurrection of those already dead. This interpretation assimilates the Corinthian Christians to the apostle's earlier opponents in I Thessalonians, who held that only those still living at the Lord's coming would be saved. Scholars who favour such a view explain Paul's question in I Corinthians 15:12 ('How can some of you say that there is no resurrection of the dead?') not so much as a flat denial of all future life, but rather as a denial of a future, *general* resurrection. This interpretation likewise suggests that verse six emphasises not that most of the five hundred are alive, but that some are already dead: 'Then he appeared to more than five hundred brethren at one time, most of whom are still alive, though some have fallen asleep.' Seemingly Paul lists this group along with the other resurrection witnesses. But actually he is deftly hinting at what he will maintain later in the chapter. Although some of these resurrection witnesses have already 'fallen asleep', they are not therefore placed at a disadvantage, let alone excluded from resurrection and a transformed future life.

Faced with this diversity of views, we should admit that no reconstruction of the opinion(s) held by Paul's opponents can claim certainty. In any case we can usefully elucidate the apostle's theology of the resurrection without necessarily relying on such a reconstruction. It is possible to focus on several answerable, if perhaps less exhilarating, questions. What role in the resurrection does Paul attribute to God? How does Paul link our resurrection with Christ's? And—our most important question—how does he understand the resurrected body? Let me take up these questions by way of an initial expedition into Paul's overall theology of the resurrection.

## THE RESURRECTOR AND THE RESURRECTEE

Rudolf Bultmann pointed out how the adjectival clause 'who raised him from the dead' became a formula-like attribute of God in Paul's letters, as well as elsewhere in the New Testament.[5] The apostle begins his letters to the Galatians with an appeal to 'God the Father who raised him [sc. Jesus] from the dead' (1:1). He warns the Corinthians against fornication by recalling their bodily destiny: 'God raised the Lord and will also raise us up by his power' (I Corinthians 6:14). Paul acknowledges that in Christ's resurrection the action was uniquely that of God (the Father). God was the resurrector, Christ the resurrectee. The only exception to Paul's normal account occurs in I Thessalonians 4:14: 'We believe that Jesus died and rose again.' Yet even here the overall stress still lies on God's intervention. The verse continues: 'Through Jesus, God will bring with him those who have fallen asleep.' In any case Paul begins the letter by reminding the Thessalonians how they 'turned to God from idols, to serve a living and true God, and wait for his Son from heaven, whom he raised from the dead' (1:9f.).

In Pauline terms God may be said simply to have raised Jesus from the dead (Romans 10:9), or to have raised him by his glory (Romans 6:4), through his Spirit (Romans 8:11) or by his power (I Corinthians 6:14). Christ's risen existence Paul calls life 'out of the power of God' (II Corinthians 13:4). This merges into the notion of this risen state being life 'for God' (Romans 6:9).

In parenthesis it is worth remarking that subsequent to Paul other New Testament authors attribute to Jesus an increasingly active role in the resurrection. Acts represents Jesus as the agent of his post-Easter appearances, albeit not yet the agent of the resurrection *tout court*: 'He presented himself after his passion' (1:3; cf. John 21:1). In the Marcan predictions of death and resurrection the Son of Man 'will rise', presumably by his own power (9:31; 10:34). This developing role for Jesus climaxes in the fourth gospel; the resurrectee becomes the resurrector. First, Jesus is the agent who will raise others (5:21ff.; 6:39–54). Second, he names himself as the agent of his own resurrection (2:19; 10:17f.). Finally, the resurrection itself is simply identified with him: 'I am the resurrection' (11:25).

To return to Paul. The apostle is, of course, not content to represent the resurrection merely as a unique intervention by God (the Father) on behalf of the dead Christ. From start to finish this resurrection deeply affects mankind.

CHRIST AND OUR RESURRECTION

In I Corinthians 15 Paul's aim obviously goes beyond simply providing testimony that Jesus of Nazareth himself had been raised from the dead, as if that were some isolated, chance fact of salvation. He also wishes to assert something greater than the mere fact that, if Christ rose, others also will rise. For Paul, this resurrection is much more than just the first case in point. Christ's victory over death proves constitutive for the resurrection of mankind, or—more strictly—of the faithful. (Paul nowhere *clearly* speaks of general resurrection, as do other New Testament authors; see John 5 : 28f.) Repeatedly Paul links the resurrection of men with that of Jesus: 'If the Spirit of him who raised Jesus from the dead dwells in you, he who raised Christ Jesus from the dead will give life to your mortal bodies also through his Spirit which dwells in you' (Romans 8 : 11). Only once does Paul refer in a generalising way to God as the one who makes the dead to live (Romans 4 : 17). He defines God as the God who has raised Christ and will raise those who die 'in Christ'. For Paul theism (as belief in the God of the resurrection) profiles belief in the risen Christ and vice versa. On the one hand, he refuses to offer a doctrine of resurrection in general—something a contemporary Pharisee might do. On the other hand, he expounds the resurrection of Christ not as an isolated privilege for one individual person, but only in its implications for other men's salvation and future destiny. Paul sees the resurrection of (at least) believers as the final and necessary consequence of God's act in raising Christ.

The apostle provides the New Testament warrant for insisting that the past resurrection of Christ can and will make no sense, unless linked with an expectation of future resurrection for ourselves. Either we hope for resurrection through assimilation to the risen body of the exalted Christ, or we cannot hope for any resurrection at all. Either we will find final happiness, complete success and ultimate freedom through Christ's resurrection, or such definitive 'wholeness' is simply unavailable. Belief in Christ's personal resurrection should be seen as tantamount to belief in a truly meaningful future for other men. From a merely human point of view the last things which may be reported both of Jesus and ourselves are the events of death and burial. If divine intervention secures victory beyond that stage, it is a victory common to other men and to Jesus as their representative. Either Christ is 'the first fruits' of those who sleep (I Corinthians 15:20) and the first-born of many brothers (Romans 8:29), or he is not risen at all. Just as the offering of the 'first fruits' (made to acknowledge God's exclusive ownership over the land of Israel and all its produce) stands for the whole harvest, so Christ's resurrection both symbolises and initiates the resurrection of others. In this strong sense he is the representative man.

At the same time the coupling of man's destiny with Christ's representative resurrection ought not to obscure the real differences. His resurrection forms a sign and promise of our resurrection, not vice versa. He alone becomes 'a life-giving spirit' (I Corinthians 15:45). His resurrection does not constitute some absolutely exact model for the rest of mankind, so that everything which should be asserted in his case holds true for other men also. Nevertheless, we may take together Christ and the rest of mankind when we ask: What is the risen body like? Paul has both cases in mind when he grapples with the questions: 'How are the dead raised? With what kind of body do they come?' (I Corinthians 15:35).

### THE RISEN BODY

Whoever like Paul maintains belief in resurrection has a great deal of explaining to do, above all with respect to the nature of the risen body. The apostle announces that our bodies will be changed at the parousia just as has already happened with Christ: 'Our commonwealth is in heaven, and from it we await a Saviour, the Lord Jesus Christ, who will change our lowly body to be like his glorious body' (Philippians 3:20f.). As such Paul refers here to the transformation of the 'survivors', those Christians who will be alive at the second coming of Christ. But right from his very first letter the apostle makes it clear that he expects both survivors and deceased to share the same change (I Thessalonians 4:13–8; I Corinthians 15:51f.). But what will this transformation be like? Can the apostle say anything useful about the risen body of Christ or the coming risen existence of other men?

Before we scrutinise Paul's doctrine of the risen body (as

expounded in I Corinthians 15:35ff. and elsewhere), two preliminary matters should be faced: the meaning of 'body' and the sources of Paul's information. First, in using 'body' (*sōma*) Paul refers to the whole man, the bodily person in his entirety, the physical human being with his possibilities of life. In these terms one should say, 'I am a body', rather than, 'I have a body'. *Sōma* means pretty well 'personal identity', 'human selfhood'. Paul can interchange at will questions dealing with the resurrection of the dead and the resurrection of the body: 'How are the *dead* raised? With what kind of *body* do they come?' (I Corinthians 15:35).

Second, where does Paul derive his information about the nature of the risen body? Probable or possible sources readily suggest themselves: (1) his Jewish heritage, (2) his Damascus-road experience, (3) the teaching offered by the pre-Pauline Christian community and, specifically, by the other official Easter witnesses, (4) special revelation(s) and (5) his reflections on scripture and his own experience. In his pre-Christian days Paul may well have understood the coming (general) resurrection to involve transformation into a glorious, 'spiritual' body. That was one Jewish interpretation of the resurrection, as we have seen. If, however, he had previously assimilated the risen body to the earthly body, the encounter on the Damascus road would have led him to abandon this material view of resurrection. One detail which could not have been derived from Jewish thought is Paul's assertion that through his resurrection Christ became a 'life-giving spirit' (I Corinthians 15:45). That a risen man should so be characterised remains foreign to Paul's Jewish background. It seems unlikely that he drew much from any teaching on the risen body offered by the pre-Pauline Christian community. We know, of course, from Galatians and Acts that Paul met Peter, James and other (earlier) official witnesses to Christ's resurrection. Certainly in I Corinthians 15:3ff. he appeals to a tradition which he had received concerning the risen Christ's appearances to such witnesses. But for the rest of the chapter he makes no use of this passage when attempting to expound the nature of the resurrection. Finally, Paul lays no claim to special revelations which have made the risen life more intelligible to him. We can safely conclude that the apostle's doctrine of the risen body arose through a reassessment of his Jewish convictions about resurrection in the light of the Damascus-road experience and his own reflections.

We draw together a great deal of Paul's doctrine by speaking of *continuity* and *transformation*. There exists, first of all, continuity. The risen man is identical with the earthly man. He remains the same human person. God makes the old creation new (Romans 8 : 21). He does not *substitute* a new creation for the old creation. It is *this* mortal body which must experience the transforming change of resurrection (I Corinthians 15 : 53; Philippians 3 : 20f.; Romans 8 : 11). There will be a personal, 'somatic' continuity between the present and the future situation. The same person who was in 'misery' will one day be in glory.

Simultaneously, resurrection means for Paul neither the reanimation of a corpse nor the reconstitution of some scattered remains, but a profound transformation, a radical, almost total difference : 'Flesh and blood cannot inherit the kingdom of God' (I Corinthians 15 : 50). Paul thinks here of the frail human nature of those who are alive, not the decayed corpses of the dead. Yet what he says applies to both living and dead : there can be no resurrection without a radical transformation of man's reality. Paul expresses this change through four antitheses (I Corinthians 15 : 43). What was subject to decay and death, 'dishonourable', weak and merely natural becomes immune to decay (through being definitively withdrawn from the threat of death in all its forms), glorious, powerful and 'spiritual'. This last adjective introduces the most significant description Paul offers. But what sense can we make of such a 'spiritual body'?

Here we need to put firmly aside the temptation to speculate about 'spiritual matter'. In choosing this adjective Paul does not have in mind the *substance* of man's bodily nature, as if through resurrection human beings were to become somehow immaterial. Rather the apostle envisions bodily existence *dominated by the Spirit* of the risen Christ instead of by all those negative, death-dealing forces which now affect man's life. Further, Paul bypasses the whole question of how man's bodily existence becomes so dominated by the Spirit. He attends only to the *result*, and leaves it to Hieronymus Bosch, Michelangelo and other artists—not to mention curious-minded theologians—to attempt to represent the *process*.[6]

How should we evaluate Paul's elucidations on the risen body of Christ and other resurrectees? At this point generalisations are perhaps inevitable and in order not to be boring must be slightly risky. It seems that the two elements of *continuity* and *transformation* stand in an almost impossible tension with one another. On the one hand, the mere reanimation of Christ's corpse would safeguard continuity excellently, but at the expense of any transformation through resurrection. (It would also absolutise the incarnation; the so-called resurrection would amount to no more than the resuscitation of the incarnate one whose earthly existence had been briefly interrupted through death on the cross.) On the other hand, the more thorough-going the transformation effected through resurrection, the more problematic becomes the task of maintaining continuity between the new risen life and the old earthly existence. The limiting case —in fact excluded by Paul—would be a totally new mode of existence. If Christ's risen life (his post-mortem bodily existence) were completely new in relation to that body crucified on Calvary and laid to rest in the tomb (his ante-mortem bodily existence), continuity of personal identity would be ruled out. The risen Christ could not be identified with the historical Jesus. A later post-mortem person would be substituted for an earlier ante-mortem person.

Even if we refuse to lose our nerve at the tension which exists between Paul's themes of transformation and continuity, these elements present a double puzzle for our imagination and understanding. We need first to find some intelligibility for the risen life itself by looking for possible descriptions. What would the life and activity of a risen man be like? The greater the transformation allowed for, the more difficult the task becomes of understanding the risen state. Sheer reanimation of a corpse (like the case of some Lazarus) is something which the human imagination can cope with. But what would a transformed, risen existence be like? If this question proves answerable, we can proceed to maintain and expound the identity between the risen man and the man who once lived and died.

One way of coping with the problem which some people adopt without too much fuss is to press the point that the divine initiative effects the risen life. God can use his sovereign power as he wills (I Corinthians 15:38). He is able to create man (I Corinthians 15:45, 48, 49) and through the resurrection bring him into a new creation, a Spirit-dominated, heavenly existence (I Corinthians 15:44ff.). God can bring about such a radical, definitive, post-mortem transformation, while somehow preserving the continuity with the earthly life of the ante-mortem person. Despite some incomprehensibility, belief in resurrected life is rendered possible through a sense of God's absolute power.

Yet matters should not be allowed to rest at the point of appeal to the divine initiative and power. Without indulging tricky theological moves it may be possible to form and fashion from the language of our world some insights into the risen life.

We can speak of the resurrection precipitating a 'new freedom for the whole person'. If by *sōma* Paul intends the human being with all his possibilities of life, the resurrection means a new, radically 'free' life. The risen man finds himself permanently liberated from all perverse, death-dealing forces, be they death itself, sin, suffering and oppression of various kinds. We may echo here the words of the young Karl Marx and speak of the resurrection overthrowing 'all conditions under which man is an oppressed, enslaved, destitute and despised being'. How far can we go in describing his new, 'glorious' existence? We can say at least this much. He has ceased to be an object in our world which can be sought out and confronted at will. As the Damascus-road event dramatically illustrates, Christ has become free to present himself or not. With sovereign freedom he initiates the episode and of his own accord emerges from his hiddenness to show himself where and to whom he wishes. Yet this fully liberated man remains identical with the old earthly man. The self survives to provide continuity, or rather not merely survives but is enhanced. Jesus continues to be fully himself in becoming different. His post-resurrection words in Luke's gospel catch this point nicely. He does not say, 'I was Jesus', still less, 'I come in place of Jesus', but he announces, 'It is I myself' (24:39).

[1] See my *Foundations of Theology* (Chicago, 1971), pp. 102–12.

[2] H. H. Rowley and W. Zimmerli have maintained—with various qualifications—that apocalyptic was the child of prophecy. G. von Rad, however, absolutely excludes this derivation and interprets apocalyptic as rooted in wisdom, thought and literature, but his view seems to be losing support. For a brief introduction to the discussion see A. M. Dubarle,

'Belief in Immortality in the Old Testament and Judaism', *Concilium*, vol. 10, no. 6 (December, 1970), pp. 34–45; P. Grelot, *The Resurrection and Modern Biblical Thought*, ed. P. de Surgy (New York, 1970), pp. 13–19; W. Zimmerli, *Man and His Hope in the Old Testament* (London and Naperville, 1970), pp. 138–50; P. D. Hanson, 'Old Testament Apocalyptic Reexamined', *Interpretation* 25 (1971), pp. 454–79.

[3] J. Blenkinsopp, 'Theological Synthesis and Hermeneutical Conclusions', *Concilium*, vol. 10, no. 6 (December, 1970), p. 123.

[4] *The Gospels Without Myth*, p. 158; italics mine.

[5] *Theology of the New Testament*, vol. 1 (London, 1952), p. 81.

[6] Not even I Thessalonians 4:13ff. and II Corinthians 5:1ff. attempt to describe this process.

# 10

# *Past, Present and Future*

In this concluding chapter I want first to explore and develop some links which Paul maintains between Christ's resurrection and the past, present and future. Such issues need not remain at a high level of generality. Specifically, how does Christ's resurrection relate theologically to the once-and-for-all event of his crucifixion on Calvary? What rôle does Paul attribute to the cross and how does Calvary affect that obedience which Christians offer to the risen Christ? Second, how does Paul link the resurrection with this present life in which Christians experience in faith the forgiveness of sins and the gift of the Holy Spirit? Third, how does the resurrection point to the coming completion of salvation? What is, so to speak, the futurity of Christ's resurrection?

## THE CRUCIFIXION

If asked to explain the relationship between resurrection and crucifixion, I have no short or easy answer to give. When presented with these central mysteries, the interpreter of Christ's life and work has a great deal of explaining to do. First things first. We face an irreversible sequence and may not go behind the resurrection to make the cross paramount. As it lacks any autonomous or absolute significance, death must be understood always in the light of Easter.

Western Christianity, however, has manifested a long-standing preoccupation with Good Friday at the expense of Easter Sunday. A complex set of causes appear to have been at work in effecting this bias in the whole tradition of the Western Church. The soul, its immortality, and man's 'inner' life came to bulk larger in the religious imagination than the resurrection of the body. A Manichean irreverence towards man's physical being also played its part here. Inevitably, a weakened interest in our resurrection implied less concern for Christ's resurrection. A neglect of the Holy Spirit went hand in hand with a deficient regard for the resurrection. In their different ways Luke, John and Paul all interpreted the Spirit in the light of the risen Christ and vice versa. The subsequent decline of pneumatology in Western Christianity inevitably entailed a weakened theology of the resurrection.

For the Pelagian elements in the Western Church, a crucifixion-oriented tendency offered more possibilities for man's spontaneous activity, whereas the resurrection confronted them with God's sovereignly free initiative. No created agent, not even Jesus's created humanity, could share in that divine intervention. Further, the individualising trend in Western theology and practice found Christ's passion and death more congenial than his resurrection. To accept the future promised through the Easter event (in which God reveals himself as the one who has raised and will raise the dead) involves us inescapably in acknowledging the resurrection as our common future. It is hardly a coincidence that in I Corinthians Paul *both* elaborates on the nature, moral responsibilities and good order of the Christian community *and* climaxes his letter with a long chapter on the resurrection.

Finally, preoccupation with the link between the Eucharist and the crucifixion, along with other polemical concerns, contributed to a neglect of the resurrection in Reformation and post-Reformation theology. Generally speaking, both Catholic and Protestant theologians have proved loyal successors to St. Anselm (1033/4–1109), who managed to discuss the redemption in his *Cur Deus homo* while completely ignoring Christ's resurrection. So long as full credit for our redemption is ascribed to Christ's death, his resurrection becomes at best a highly useful (if not strictly necessary) proof of Christian claims. Looking back on much Western theology we might parody Paul and cry out: 'Resurrection is swallowed up in crucifixion. O Resurrection, where is thy victory? O Resurrection, where is thy sting?' Against this historical background it occasions little surprise to find that so many religious orders and congregations have drawn their names from Jesus's sufferings and death (Passionists, Stigmatines, Society of Precious Blood, etc.), but hardly any from the resurrection itself. There are few Fathers of the Resurrection, Institutes of Easter or Sisters of the Empty Tomb. The bias has affected Western art, as well as piety. Hugh Anderson relates how 'Michelangelo once broke out in indignant protest against his fellow-artists because they were forever depicting Christ in his death on the Cross. "Paint him instead", he cried, "the Lord of life; paint him with his kingly feet planted on the stone that held him in the tomb." ' Anderson comments: 'The artist was true to the New Testament. The New Testament, for all its emphasis on Jesus's passion and death, will not allow us to stop short at the Cross.'[1] But, of course, Michelangelo continued to depict Christ's death from that early Pietà in St. Peter's to that much more poignant Pietà in the Florence Duomo. His statue of the risen Christ in the Sopra Minerva in Rome is not what draws visitors to that church. In this case, even Michelangelo hardly put his hands where his mouth was.

In the face of Western Christianity's preoccupation with Good Friday it must be stressed that the death of Jesus lacks autonomous significance. However, we may not go to the other extreme and underplay the enormous significance it does possess. Otherwise our very account of the resurrection will be essentially impoverished. Peter Steele remarks in an unpublished paper: 'It is only if the crucifixion—Christ crucified—is seen as unspeakably outrageous—a situation more squalid and grotesque than one can get straight in words—that there can be any truly good news here at all. If the crucifixion does not become more stunning the more one contemplates it, the resurrection is going to be just a gaudy tail-piece to a hard-luck story.'

Among New Testament authors Luke stands out as the one who plays down somewhat the horror and significance of Jesus's crucifixion. Far from being a stumbling-block (I Corinthians 1:23), the cross is presented by Luke as something natural, preordained and only to be expected by those who recognised God's purposes. 'Was it not necessary that the Christ should suffer these things and enter into his glory?' (Luke 24:26; cf. vss. 7, 44). In his passion story Luke depicts Jesus as suffering in the manner of a righteous man and like Stephen dying a martyr's death. Surrounded by weeping women and 'the good thief' (23:27ff., 40ff.), Jesus expires with a prayer of confidence on his lips ('Father, into thy hands I commit my spirit') rather than the Marcan cry of dereliction ('My God, my God, why hast thou forsaken me?'). In quieter, tamer accents Luke describes the honourable death of a wholly innocent person. As a consequence the astonishing nature of the resurrection is partially muted. In Mark the women flee from the empty tomb, terrified and silent before God's unique intervention on behalf of the crucified Jesus (16:8). Luke, however, portrays these women as remembering Jesus's prediction of his death and resurrection and quietly returning to the apostles with the news of their discovery (24:8f.).

This characterisation of Luke demands, of course, modifications. For one thing he does represent the risen Jesus as still bearing in his body the signs of his passion: 'See my hands and my feet, that it is I myself' (24:39). The risen Lord who suddenly stands among his disciples should be identified precisely through the marks of the crucifixion. The cross qualifies the resurrection. This motif appears also in the Johannine narrative. Jesus not only shows his disciples 'his hands and his side', but also invites Thomas to touch the marks of his passion: 'Put your finger here, and see my hands; and put out your hand, and place it in my side' (John 20:20, 27; cf. 19:34). In the fourth gospel the remembrance of the crucifixion qualifies the resurrection story. When the risen Christ appears to Peter and entrusts him with the task of feeding his 'lambs and sheep', he also predicts the suffering and death which Peter must be ready to face. ' "When you are old, you will stretch out your hands, and another will gird you and carry you where you do not wish to go." This he said to show by what death he was to glorify God' (John 21:18f.). The Easter encounter forms no ecstatic idyll. The prospect of service and suffering colours the joy of this meeting with the victorious Christ.

To come back to Paul. For his part, the apostle never forgets that the resurrected Christ remains the same person as the crucified Jesus. The theme of his preaching is 'Christ crucified'. He does not attempt to reverse the Calvary-Easter sequence. But he refuses to play down the enormous import of the crucifixion. The apostle's thought goes far beyond mere recollection of the risen

Christ's past history. The crucifixion is not remembered simply because Jesus had to face Calvary en route to his resurrection. We are dealing with something much greater than mere respectful tribute to a painful episode once endured by the object of Paul's devoted service. The risen Christ became and remains Redeemer only through his death. The resurrection proved the saving event for the world because of its connection with the death on Calvary. Since Christ 'was put to death for our trespasses', he could be 'raised for our justification' (Romans 4 : 25).

The resurrection would not have saved men and restored them to a proper covenant relationship with God, unless Christ had first been handed over 'for our sins'. This last phrase brings us to the meaning of Christ's death which Pauline theology expounds. Matthew, Mark and Luke show themselves interested primarily in the *fact* of Jesus's death, not in its redemptive value. Further, the Synoptic predictions of the passion ascribe the responsibility for the crucifixion to a limited set of people. 'And he [sc. Jesus] began to teach them that the Son of man must suffer many things, and be rejected by the elders and the chief priests and the scribes, and be killed, and after three days rise again' (Mark 8 : 31; cf. 10 : 33f.). But for Paul (who draws here on traditional formulations from the Christian community), Christ was handed over 'for *our* sins'. The community confesses thus its sinfulness and the expiatory value of Christ's death on its behalf.

We can distinguish various levels of explanation. (1) The crucifixion carries a saving, beneficial value *for others*: 'He [sc. God] did not spare his own Son but gave him up for us all' (Romans 8 : 32). (2) This death atones for and rescues *sinners*: 'Christ died for the ungodly' (Romans 5 : 6); he 'gave himself for our sins to deliver us from the present evil age' (Galatians 1 : 4). (3) It is not simply a just man who suffered death for our sins, but the *Messiah* himself: 'Christ died for our sins' (I Corinthians 15 : 3). At times Paul expresses the atoning, expiatory value of Christ's crucifixion as a death 'for us', 'for us all', 'for me' and 'for the ungodly'. At other times he appeals to the representative nature of this death : 'One has died *for all*; therefore *all* have died. And he died for all, that those who live might live no longer for themselves but for him who for their sake died and was raised' (II Corinthians 5 : 14f.). Yet the redemption was not complete on Good Friday. The scandal of Paul's good news goes beyond the claim that the Messiah's death on Calvary atoned for the past sins of mankind. For this crucified man conveyed God's *promised future* to the world.

*Both* the death of Jesus *and* his resurrection brought salvation. If I Corinthians 15:3 refers explicitly only to the redemptive value of the crucifixion, Romans 4:25 includes also the resurrection. Both Good Friday and Easter Sunday resulted in a new life communicated to Christians through faith and baptism. Paul appears reluctant to express this salvific work of Christ in the vaguer terms of humiliation and exaltation. He describes the redemptive events precisely and concretely as crucifixion and resurrection.

## RISING WITH CHRIST

The fact that Paul associates both crucifixion and resurrection in Christ's saving work could lead us to the false conclusion that he considers the faithful to participate equally now in this dying and rising. Paul reminds the Roman Christians that baptism is a sacramental assimilation to Christ's death: 'Do you not know that all of us who have been baptised into Christ Jesus were baptised into his death? We were buried therefore with him by baptism into death, so that as Christ was raised from the dead by the glory of the Father, we too might walk in newness of life' (6:3f.). This passage has led many commentators, not to mention unwary readers, to speak of the Christian as dead *and risen* with Christ. This is precisely what Paul declines to say. His parallel runs: 'As Christ was raised from the dead, so we walk in newness of life.' He refuses to write: 'As Christ was raised from the dead, so we too are raised.' Rather the apostle affirms: 'If we have been united with him in a death like his, we *shall* certainly be united with him in a resurrection like his' (6:5). Through faith and baptism Christians enjoy a new life and freedom from sin, in the sense that baptism calls them to new obedience. 'Our old self was crucified with him so that . . . we might no longer be enslaved to sin' (6:6). But they remain capable of submitting again to the rule of sin. The last enemy, death, has still to be overcome (I Corinthians 15:26). Death can still destroy man through sin. Resurrection remains an object of Christian hope. At best it can be anticipated by that 'newness of life', the obedient conduct of those freed from the tyranny of sin. But further than this Paul will not go. Christians still live under the shadow of the crucifixion and have not yet risen definitively with Christ. Certainly the author(s) of Ephesians and Colossians show themselves ready to portray Christian initiation as a dying *and rising* with Christ,[2] but not Paul. For him the sign of the cross expresses the fact that Christians must still hope for the completion of their salvation. Christ's own victory has already been effected in his resurrection, but for other men the proper participation in his resurrection has not yet taken place. The apostle may apply the term '(new) life' to the present existence of the faithful, but reserves 'resurrection' either to Christ's own resurrection or to other men's *future* resurrection.

In the Pauline language of redemption verbs associating us 'with' Christ play a prominent role. We 'suffer' with Christ, are 'crucified' with him, 'die' with him and are 'buried' with him. But the parallelism breaks down at the point of the resurrection. The authentic Paul never maintains that 'we now rise or have already risen with Christ', but only that 'we believe that we *shall* live with him' (Romans 6 : 8).

### SALVATION PRESENT AND FUTURE

While personal resurrection remains a matter of hope, there are saving realities presently experienced—faith, the forgiveness of sins and the gift of the Holy Spirit. These realities inaugurate the future, so that to deny our coming resurrection would be tantamount to rejecting not only Christ's resurrection but also the present experience of faith and forgiveness (I Corinthians 15 : 16f.). To know the indwelling Spirit is to believe that this gift promises complete new life through future resurrection: 'If the Spirit of him who raised Jesus from the dead dwells in you, he who raised Christ Jesus from the dead will give life to your mortal bodies also through his Spirit which dwells in you' (Romans 8 : 11). Paul makes his primary appeal to this experience of the Holy Spirit. In Galatians the opening insistence on the authoritative origin of his gospel which 'came through a revelation of Jesus Christ' (1 : 12) should not distract us from his basic argument: 'Let me ask you only this: Did you receive the Spirit by works of the law, or by hearing with faith?' (3 : 2; cf. 4 : 29–5 : 25). The Spirit sent by the risen Christ functions as a pledge of that total justification through future resurrection: 'Through the Spirit, by faith, we wait for the hope of righteousness' (Galatians 5:5). In Philippians Paul expresses his deepest wish that 'I may know him [sc. Christ] and the power of his resurrection, and may share his sufferings, becoming like him in his death, that if possible I may attain the resurrection from the dead' (3:10f.). Put concretely, knowing Christ in the power of his resurrection is experiencing now the Spirit given by the risen Christ.

If Paul appeals primarily to the present experience of the Holy Spirit, he interprets it within the horizon of the future. Christians experience the Spirit provisionally, as bearing witness not only that the earthly Jesus died and was raised but also that he is *yet to come*. The saving events of Christ's death and resurrection, appropriated in faith, have opened up for Paul the perspective of the final triumph for Christ in the resurrection of the dead and transformation of the world. Thus the resurrection transcends the past and present by assigning a certain priority to what has *not yet* happened, the advent of God's future. The resurrection promises man and his world a supreme enhancement, not a mere repetition of what they already are.

First of all, this eschatological hope is *Christian*, no longer the kind of Pharisaic expectation of general resurrection which Luke attributes to Paul in Acts 24:14f.[3] The resurrection of Jesus has transmuted Paul's perspective on the final events. In expecting such a future he adopts that relation to the future which faith in Christ requires (I Corinthians 15:14). Second, because it is Christ who has been raised, Paul's perspective becomes universal: 'As in Adam all die, so also in Christ shall all be made alive' (I Corinthians 15:22; cf. vv. 21–28). Even though in that chapter Paul concerns himself with the faithful who die 'in Christ' and fails to speak literally of the resurrection of non-Christians as well as Christians, nevertheless the implication of a general resurrection is there.

Third, Paul's perspective takes on cosmic proportions. He has moved from his own individual experience ('Have I not seen Jesus our Lord?') to that vision of the end when Christ 'must reign until he has put all his enemies under his feet', so that eventually 'God may be everything to every one' (I Corinthians 9:1; 15:25, 28). The material creation too waits 'with eager longing' for liberation and transformation with man in the future resurrection (Romans 8:19ff.). There will be a transformed world for a resurrected mankind. Without question Paul's cosmic eschatology to which both Christ's resurrection itself and the experience of the Spirit direct him remains highly obscure. Just as we cannot immediately 'get at' Christ's past resurrection, so we cannot comprehend either our own coming resurrection or the future resurrection of the world. We must cope not only with a temporal gap but also with an ignorance of the inner nature of such resurrection.

But assuredly Paul deals with a final future *of* our history and world, not a utopian future *in* our history and world. It is God who will make all things new and bring back into being that which once was but no longer is. The transformation of man and his world may not be fitted into a merely evolutionary scheme of natural causality. Paul knows of only one cause for this coming resurrection—God (I Corinthians 15:38), or Christ (Philippians 3:20f.) or God acting through his Spirit (Romans 8:11). This universal transfiguration, inaugurated by the resurrection of Jesus, forms no mere organic movement in a world process but reveals the unique, creative power of God. The divine power has begun to liberate man from his accumulated suffering and make the world new at the end of the ages.

To sum up. God has revealed himself in Jesus Christ as the God who has raised and will raise the dead. Paul's perspective on the coming intervention of God takes the form of a Christian, universal, even cosmic hope.

### THE PRIOR AND POSTERIOR MYSTERIES

Paul's treatment of Christ's resurrection manages to integrate up to a point themes of past, present and future. He links the once-and-for-all death on Calvary to Christian experience of the Holy Spirit which promises that which is yet to come, the resurrection of the dead and the transformation of man's world. Against the background of this Pauline theology I propose to round off this chapter by drawing attention to a long-standing and widespread failure among theologians to achieve anything like an adequate view of the resurrection in relation to the other great Christological themes. Let us agree to use the word 'mysteries'. From the central point of Christ's resurrection there are the *prior* mysteries (creation, incarnation, the ministry and the crucifixion), and the *posterior* mysteries (the exaltation, Pentecost, the birth of the Church and the *parousia*). Theologians, where they have discussed the resurrection, have exhibited a remarkable tendency to absorb the resurrection 'backwards' or 'forwards'. Consistently they have eroded the significance of the resurrection by collapsing it into either the prior or the posterior Christological mysteries. Let me illustrate my case in detail.

The resurrection may be drawn 'backwards' by reducing it in favour of an all-inclusive theology of the *incarnation*. Karl Rahner exemplifies this tendency. When he—along with many other theologians—describes the incarnation as the 'climax' in 'the total history of the human race', it is scarcely surprising to find him arguing that 'in virtue of the inmost essence of the incarnation, seen as a formally salvific act, the one event composed of death and resurrection, is implied and accepted'.[4] In brief, 'the resurrection . . . can be adequately understood only in reference to the absolute mystery of the incarnation'.[5] Of course, such an incarnation-centred theology not only finds representatives among contemporary theologians like Rahner and, as we have seen, Lampe, but goes back a long way in the history of Christianity. This kind of theology often took popular expression in such a hypothetical statement as: 'When God became man, any single episode of suffering or even any single deed of obedience would have been enough to have saved mankind.' In those terms, the death and resurrection of Christ—not to mention a recognisable human life and history—would be dispensed with, because the incarnation *as such* has assumed supreme, almost unique, theological significance.

In the early Church many writers, in particular the Greek fathers like Athanasius or Cyril of Alexandria, stated matters not hypothetically, but positively: 'God became man in order that man might become God.' In such formulations the incarnation took on the role of *the* redeeming and divinising event. The death and resurrection of Christ were bypassed.[6] The same theology surfaces in the opening chapter of John: 'The Word became flesh and dwelt among us, full of grace and truth; we have beheld his glory, glory as of the only Son from the Father . . . And from his fulness have we all received, grace upon grace' (1:14, 16). The evangelist here presents the incarnation as the primary factor in Christian salvation. Where a theology *begins* with the notion of Christ's pre-existence, it is likely to interpret as *the* saving event the incarnation rather than Christ's death and resurrection. That holds true of John and the Greek Fathers, but not of Paul. Of course, the apostle does from time to time speak of the Son's pre-existence (Galatians 4:4; Romans 8:3), but he takes the incarnation to be a *prerequisite* to the redemptive work. Paul makes Christ's saving death and resurrection his starting-point. Here he finds the climax of the whole history of the human race and, if he were to use such a term, the 'absolute' Christological mystery.

Another way of eroding the significance of the resurrection has been to underplay it in favour of Jesus's *ministry*. At the risk of obscuring their far-reaching differences, we can lump together here such diverse theologians as Paul van Buren, Gerhard Ebeling, Ernst Fuchs, Lloyd Geering and Willi Marxsen. In chapter three we saw how van Buren interprets the Easter events to mean that after the crucifixion the disciples received a new perspective upon the historical Jesus, so that they became infected with a 'measure of the freedom which had been Jesus's during his life'. In other words, the example and teaching of Jesus eventually had its effect by inspiring the disciples to be 'men for others'. Thus the ministry of Jesus assumes for van Buren a (? unique) importance in freeing those men who hear Jesus's message.

Ebeling and his friend Fuchs likewise stress the ministry at the expense of the resurrection. For them man's salvation essentially consists in coming to believe *like* the historical Jesus, who was the 'representative of faith' (Fuchs) or the 'witness of faith' (Ebeling). In terms that van Buren might have used Ebeling writes: 'The faith of the days after Easter knows itself to be nothing else but the right understanding of the Jesus of the days before Easter . . . To believe in Jesus therefore means: to enter into relations with God in view of him, to let him give us the freedom to believe.'[7] He concludes:

> His [sc. Jesus's] work of bringing certainty to men was completed when he died abandoned by God and men. Now we may be tempted to misconstrue the fact that, seemingly, Jesus himself aroused only little faith—and that very weak—until

> after his death. We may say that what Jesus was unable to achieve, was furnished by the additional fact of his resurrection, as if the post-resurrection faith was something other than the consequence of Jesus's certainty. But this would be to turn away from the certainty of faith of the historical Jesus.[8]

Fuchs develops the theme of Jesus's consciousness of God's presence which led him to call men to love. Jesus decided, if needs be, to die for that proclamation. The consequence follows: 'To have faith in Jesus now means essentially to repeat Jesus's decision', to share his self-understanding.[9] Thus the existentialist interpretation of Fuchs and Ebeling accounts for redemption by maximalising the effect of the historical Jesus's freedom and faith. They drastically downgrade the resurrection by retreating to the preaching situation of the ministry.

Geering in his own way allows the resurrection to be swallowed up by the life (and death) of Jesus. He argues that the apostles 'must have wrestled with the "offence" of the cross, in the light of the teaching of Jesus and of their memory of all that he had been'. Thus they 'came to believe that death could not overpower a life of this quality'. So Jesus's death 'did not bring to an end his power to attract men and to lead them to a new life', but his power to encourage lives devoid of self-interest was experienced more fully and widely.[10] In short, the post-crucifixion situation witnessed the disciples at long last gathering inspiration and courage from the example of Jesus's heroic life and death.

Finally, we have noted in chapter six how Marxsen emphasises the call of the historical Jesus to make the venture of faith. In this way 'the cause of Jesus' goes on. We can hear his message to 'see through the circumscription of our lives', to allow 'tomorrow's worries belong to tomorrow', to 'seek out the other person instead of defending ourselves from him'.

In all these interpretations the ministry of Jesus assumes central significance. Let me put matters in extreme terms. It would make little difference, if at the end of his ministry Jesus had suddenly disappeared and had never been seen again. Provided that his words along with some indications of his unselfish conduct had been preserved, men could venture faith, share Jesus's self-understanding and live free lives devoid of self-concern. The resurrection and even the cross have no integral part to play in the theologies of Fuchs, Ebeling, Geering, Marxsen and van Buren.

Other theologians have manifested yet another deficient trend by collapsing Easter Sunday 'backwards' into Good Friday, or simply ignoring the resurrection because they were engrossed with the crucifixion. We have commented above on such a long-standing bias in Western theology. Among recent writers Bultmann exemplifies this preoccupation by (1) allowing the resurrection no independent status as a further event subsequent to the crucifixion, and (2) interpreting it as an expression of the meaningfulness of the cross. What is released through the Easter proclamation is nothing else but the message of the cross, the signification of the crucifixion 'for me'.[11]

So far we have briefly reviewed some ways in which Christ's resurrection has been absorbed 'backwards' into prior 'mysteries'. The movement can also run in the opposite direction, if theologians erode the momentous value of Easter Sunday in favour of present Christian experience, the coming *parousia* or other posterior 'mysteries'. Evely illustrates one such way of eroding the status of Christ's resurrection. He so dotes upon its present resonances in our experience, the signals of resurrection, that he plumps for a form of realised, present eschatology. He warns his readers: 'We must not project our religion into the past or into the future. It matters little whether Christ *rose* from the dead. What matters is that he *is* risen. It is of no importance whether we ourselves will rise on the last day; it is important that we are risen and that we are in eternal life.' In brief, 'the most important resurrection of all is the one that we experience'.[12]

Yet another way of reducing Christ's resurrection into posterior 'mysteries' has surfaced among various apocalyptic sects. They have frequently overemphasised the future coming of Christ at the expense of what has been effected through the resurrection. This was to underplay the 'already' in favour of the 'not yet', if one may pirate yet once more Oscar Cullmann's terminology. However, the mere fact of attention to the coming end can be deceptive. The question must be answered with all seriousness: 'How new will be the new creation?' A given theologian may in fact relate the *eschaton* (the ultimate posterior mystery) so closely to the original creation (the original prior mystery) that essentially he robs time, history, evil and suffering—quite apart from the startlingly new event of Christ's resurrection itself—of their proper significance. Bultmann, if I may leave aside some needed qualifications, relates *eschaton* and creation in such an unacceptably close fashion. Through hearing the word of proclamation man can take the decision of faith, which has among other things two effects. In Bultmannian terms he finds authentic, 'eschatological' existence. ('Eschatological' here denotes an eternal 'now', which is ultimate in importance rather than ultimate in time.) Simultaneously he emerges from a state of forgetfulness to acknowledge his real origin as a creature of God. Achieving one's personal *eschaton*, so to speak, means precisely recovering a consciousness of creation.[13]

Let these examples suffice to illustrate what I mean by absorbing Christ's resurrection 'backwards' or 'forwards' into prior or posterior Christological mysteries. Such deficient theological tendencies contrast with Paul's determination not to allow the proper relations between the resurrection and other key Christological themes to become dissolved. In the apostle's circumstances that meant battling on two fronts. On the one hand, the remembrance of the past crucifixion must remain alive. The present experience of the exalted Lord should not obscure the fact that he is the same person as the crucified Jesus. On the other hand, the present gift of the Spirit enjoys a provisional nature. It points forward to the object of Christian hope, the resurrection. Neither past nor future may be suppressed in favour of some timeless present, even a present filled with a sense of the risen and exalted Christ.

[1] *Jesus and Christian Origins* (New York, 1964), p. 185.

[2] Colossians 2:12 reads: 'You were buried with him in baptism, in which you were also raised with him through faith in the working of God, who raised him from the dead'; see also Ephesians 2:5f. In Colossians the object of hope is *future glory* (3:4).

[3] Geering glosses over the Christological quality which radically changed Paul's resurrection hope: 'On the subject of the general resurrection to come there is no fundamental break between Jewish thought and Christian thought. The Christians *simply inherited* this form of their future hope from their Jewish heritage' (*Resurrection*, p. 127; italics mine).

[4] *Theological Investigations*, IV (London and Baltimore, 1966), pp. 130, 185.

[5] *Theological Dictionary* (New York, 1965), p. 407.

[6] See J. P. Jossua, *Le salut, incarnation ou mystère pascal* (Paris, 1968).
[7] *Word and Faith* (London, 1963), p. 302.
[8] *Theology and Proclamation* (London and Philadelphia, 1966), p. 91.
[9] *Studies of the Historical Jesus* (London and Naperville, 1964), p. 28.
[10] *Resurrection*, pp. 139, 226, 228.
[11] *Kerygma and Myth*, p. 41.
[12] *The Gospels Without Myth*, pp. 154, 157.
[13] *Existence and Faith* (London and Cleveland, 1960), p. 85f.

# *Postscript*

THIS BOOK HAS dealt with Christ's resurrection from the standpoint of history, belief and theology. We attempted first to clarify the historical origins and meaning of the basic Easter message found in I Corinthians 15:3–8 and the resurrection narratives in the four gospels. We reached the conclusion that two originally independent and substantially reliable traditions constituted the historical kernel behind these texts. On the one hand, the risen Christ appeared (perhaps in Galilee) to individuals and groups. On the other hand, one or more women independently of these appearances discovered his tomb to be empty on the third day.

After settling the content and character of the essential New Testament witness to Christ's resurrection, we raised the question of belief. What is involved in accepting or rejecting this testimony? There it was argued that *both* past witness *and* present experience contribute to Easter faith. Assent to the truth of Jesus's resurrection combines knowledge of past reports with an interpretation of present experience. Personal and social expectations constitute the context in which the apostolic testimony can be understood and appropriated. This is not learning to whistle in the dark in a spirit of bland optimism. Rather, through discovering a degree of purpose and coherence in 'my' life, I can accept the promise conveyed by witness to Christ's resurrection. In the face of death and concomitant evils, God will vindicate his word and bring the new creation of resurrection.

Finally, after scrutinising the resurrection theology of the gospels, we offered some theological elucidations on the empty tomb and the resurrection 'body'. We concluded by developing those links in Paul's resurrection doctrine between resurrection and the past (the crucifixion) and the future (the *parousia*), which prevent the resurrection from being either isolated from or absorbed into other Christological mysteries.

Thus the procedure adopted began with historico-literary questions, turned to issues of faith and ended with some theological reflections. Another tripartite approach which my friend George Hunsinger suggested in an unpublished paper[1] would cover in turn the ontology, epistemology and hermeneutics of Christ's resurrection. What was and/or is the resurrection in the order of being—in its status as an historical event? How do we know about it? How do we translate our Easter texts into statements of present significance? In such a scheme we would move from the order of being to the order of knowledge and then the task of finding significant language which would illuminate God's action in overcoming evil through resurrection. This tripartite scheme of ontology, epistemology and hermeneutics offers some equivalence to my division of history, faith and theology.

We should now be in a clearer position to affirm and interpret that statement with which I refused to begin: 'Christianity stands or falls with the reality of Jesus's resurrection from the dead.' In a profound sense Christianity without the resurrection is not simply Christianity without its final chapter. It is not Christianity at all. As we have noted, to deny the resurrection amounts in Paul's eyes to a denial of Christian faith itself.

Yet much, if not everything, depends on what a given author means by 'resurrection' or the 'reality' of Christ's resurrection. Among others van Buren, Geering and Evely exemplify mutilated interpretations of that reality. Van Buren reduces the resurrection to a radical post-crucifixion change in the disciples. Jesus's freedom finally proves contagious in their regard.

Geering may think he is grappling with the question of Jesus's resurrection, but his fist closes on something else, what he calls the 'idiom of the resurrection'. He summarises his thesis as follows:

> Eternal life does not mean the endless prolongation of a conscious self, but a life of such quality that, having no further

> concern for self-interest, can transcend death and rise to a fresh mode of manifestation in the lives of men who follow. *It is in this sense that Christians use the idiom of resurrection* to confess their faith in Jesus and say that God raised him from the dead.[2]

Very many Christians would disagree with Geering's bland assertion that 'this is the sense' in which they accept Jesus and his resurrection. Moreover, why obscure matters with an ambiguous 'idiom of the resurrection' which has to be unpacked in such a way? Would it not suffice to observe that the power and influence of generous men can survive their passing and, given a death of heroic quality, may even be enhanced by such a death? We find, of course, this commonplace turning up everywhere in literature, both Christian and non-Christian, ancient and modern. We meet it, for instance, in an essay on the choice of a vocation which the young Karl Marx wrote for his final school examination in August 1835. Marx concluded on a romantic note:

> History names those men as the greatest who ennobled themselves in that they worked for the common good. Experience praises as the happiest man the one who has made the most people happy. Religion itself teaches us that the Ideal whom all emulate offered himself for mankind. Who would dare to cancel out such sayings? If we have chosen the position in which we can best work for mankind, then burdens cannot depress us, since we are only an offering for all people. Then we will enjoy no petty, restricted, egotistical joy, but our happiness will belong to millions. Our deeds will live on quietly, but continually effective forever, and our ashes will be moistened by the burning tears of noble men.[3]

In the case of Jesus it is indisputable that his message and example have been 'continually effective' through the centuries. But millions have been deceived and I am wildly misreading the New Testament, if no claim is made that there existed and exists a living person behind that message. I may reject that claim and maintain that Jesus died, remained dead and cannot confront me today as a living person. In that case I would prefer—provided Marx's noble men would allow me into their ranks—to let my burning tears fall on his tomb in Highgate cemetery rather than on some putative grave in the Jerusalem Church of the Holy Sepulchre.

Lastly, Evely prejudges the issue of the resurrection by restricting the possibilities of divine activity on behalf of mankind. He asserts that 'we can find God only in our own experience', not in 'an event of the past' or through 'long-dead witnesses'.[4] Such theologising in alternatives characterises much of *The Gospels Without Myth*. Evely simply rules out in advance certain positions, in this case that we can discover the risen Christ *both* through our own experience *and* through the word of long-dead apostles who testified to past encounters with their resurrected Lord. Like some wines such theology can neither mature in its native France nor travel well abroad.

Of course, theologians have never shown themselves immune against possible capitulation to the prevailing *Zeitgeist*. The history of Christianity is littered with examples of those who fell victim to the prejudices and fashions of their age. Hence it should occasion no surprise to find some contemporary theologians giving ground or even surrendering to the widespread incredulity about personal life beyond death. The one who maintains that God brought Jesus back to life in a resurrection which anticipates the final transformation of man and his world can seem to lack integrity. It looks as if he is struggling to fabricate a case which will enable him to retain a traditional belief that ought to be abandoned or at least radically reinterpreted. That kind of manipulation of the Easter message, however, represents loss rather than gain. R. R. Niebuhr rightly observes:

> The resurrection of Christ has been allegorised and volatilised in nearly every imaginable way, but the fact remains that neither Jesus himself nor the Christian community can manifest a distinctive character or true identity apart from the resurrection event itself, where faith, hope and love are given their vindication and new birthright.[5]

Without the resurrection Christians can hardly suffer an essentially Christian identity crisis, because they will have little or no Christian identity.

In a sense the sceptics and rationalists have proved unexpected allies from earliest times. Celsus, David Hume and the rest appreciated enough of the Christian proclamation about the resurrection to know that some extraordinary claim was being made, and not some banal assertion that the influence of an unselfish man can survive and grow after his death. In the name of reason and good sense they rejected this claim, but they paid it the implicit respect of acknowledging its prodigious nature. They refused to allow that a resurrection-shaped hole had been punched through the fabric of human history.

But ultimately sheer reason and good sense alone prove here neither decisive nor final. In the closing chapters of John's gospel it is the 'beloved' disciple who shows himself sensitively aware of his risen Lord's presence. There exists a deep connection between love and knowledge—a connection denied by the peculiarly modern prejudice that love is blind. According to that prejudice all true knowledge can come only through the careful control of our feelings so that we can proceed with scientific objectivity to supposedly sound conclusions. Love, however, does recognise the truth, as Augustine, Goethe, Dostoevski and others have appreciated in their different ways. 'Give me a lover,' cried Augustine, 'and he will understand.' The young Goethe wrote: 'We learn to know only what we love. The depth and fullness of our knowledge are proportionate to the strength, vigour and liveliness of our love and even our passion.' It was a reflection that Goethe would repeat and explore through a lifetime. The most cursory glance at the closing pages of Dostoevski's *Crime and Punishment* reveals the heavy use of resurrection imagery, as love brings Raskolnikoff to acknowledge the reality of his existence. Under the impact of Sonia's devotion the hero finally accepts the truth about himself and her. In a genuine sense only lovers have their eyes opened and can see the truth.[6]

With respect to resurrection faith sheer reason and good sense alone fail to prove decisive. Nor are they final. One has belief in the risen Christ without fully understanding the resurrection. It is like believing in someone's love. You can say a lot, although you can say very little conclusively.

If the heart has its reasons and love enables man to recognise reality, the lover also knows that he can never exhaust the truth about the object of his love. He knows that it may be better to say too little than too much. There is a time to fall silent like those friends of Gandalf when the old man quite unexpectedly returned: 'Between wonder, joy and fear they stood and found no words to say.'[7] Christ's resurrection remains far more than the sum of any or all descriptions of it. At some point we will find no words to say. Then we can do no more than pay silent homage to the awesome nature of this resurrection from the dead, the beginning of God's new creation.

[1] 'The Daybreak of the New Creation: Christ's Resurrection as an Eschatological Event'.

[2] *Resurrection*, p. 232f.; italics mine.

[3] *Werke*, I, *Frühe Schriften*, ed. H. J. Lieber and P. Furth (Darmstadt, 1962), p. 5; translation my own.

[4] *The Gospels Without Myth*, pp. 102, 148.

[5] *Resurrection and Historical Reason* (New York, 1957), p. v.

[6] For references and further discussion see M. Scheler, 'Liebe und Erkenntnis', *Gesammelte Werke*, VI (Munich, 1963), pp. 77–98.

[7] J. R. Tolkien, *The Lord of the Rings*, II, *The Two Towers* (London, 1954), p. 98.

# *Select Bibliography*


E. L. Bode, *The First Easter Morning. The Gospel Accounts of the Women's Visit to the Tomb of Jesus* (Rome, 1970).

R. E. Brown, *The Virginal Conception and Bodily Resurrection of Jesus* (London and New York, 1973), pp. 69–129.

H. von Campenhausen, *Tradition and Life in the Church* (London and Philadelphia, 1968), pp. 43–89.

J. D. G. Dunn, *Jesus and the Spirit* (London, 1975), pp. 95–134.

C. F. Evans, *Resurrection and the New Testament* (London and Naperville, 1970).

R. H. Fuller, *The Formation of the Resurrection Narratives* (London, 1971).

J. P. Galvin, 'The Resurrection of Jesus in Catholic Systematics', *Heythrop Journal* 20 (1979), pp. 123–45.

J. P. Jossua, *Le Salut, incarnation ou mystère pascal* (Paris, 1968).

W. Kasper, *Jesus the Christ* (London and New York, 1976), pp. 124–60.

B. Klappert (ed.), *Diskussion um Kreuz und Auferstehung* (Wuppertal, 1967).

X. Léon-Dufour, *Resurrection and the Message of Easter* (London, 1974).

W. P. Loewe, 'The Appearances of the Risen Lord : Faith, Fact and Objectivity', *Horizons* 6 (1979), pp. 177–92.

W. Marxsen, *The Resurrection of Jesus of Nazareth* (London and Philadelphia, 1970).

J. Moltmann, *The Crucified God* (London and New York, 1974).

——, *Theology of Hope* (London and New York, 1967), pp. 139–229.

G. O'Collins, *What are they saying about the Resurrection?* (New York, 1978).

W. Pannenberg, *Jesus – God and Man* (London and Philadelphia, 1968), pp. 53–114.

N. Perrin, *The Resurrection Narratives* (London, 1977).

K. Rahner, 'The Theology of the Death and the Resurrection of Jesus', *Foundations of Christian Faith* (London and New York, 1978), pp. 264–85.

E. Schillebeeckx, *Jesus* (London and New York, 1979), pp. 320–97, 516–44.

P. Selby, *Look for the Living* (London, 1976).

M. E. Thrall, 'Resurrection Traditions in Christian Apologetic', *Thomist* 43 (1979), pp. 197–216.

H. Wansbrough, *Risen from the Dead* (Slough, 1978).

R. C. Ware, 'The Resurrection of Jesus', *Heythrop Journal* 16 (1975), pp. 22–35, 174–94.

U. Wilckens, *Resurrection* (Edinburgh, 1977).

H. Williams, *True Resurrection* (New York, 1974).

*Note*: As it happens, I have reviewed some of the books listed in this bibliography. It may be worth indicating the whereabouts of those reviews. A forthcoming review of Schillebeeckx's work has already been noted in the new preface.

*Gregorianum* 56 (1975), pp. 584–5 (Léon-Dufour).

*What are they saying about the Resurrection?*, pp. 106–15 (Marxsen); reprinted from *Heythrop Journal* 12 (1971), pp. 207–11.

*Interpretation* 22 (1968), pp. 36–52 (Moltmann's *Theology of Hope*).

*Interpretation* 23 (1969), pp. 228–32 (Pannenberg).

*Heythrop Journal* 18 (1977), pp. 466–7 (Perrin).

*Heythrop Journal* 20 (1979), pp. 192–4 (Wansbrough).

# *Index of Names*